Immaterial World

Transparency in Architecture
Marc Kristal

THE MONACELLI PRESS

Library of Congress Cataloging-in-Publication Data
Kristal, Marc.
Immaterial world : transparency in architecture / Marc Kristal.—1st ed.
p. cm.
ISBN 978-1-58093-314-8 (hardcover)
1. Architecture, Modern—21st century—Themes, motives.
2. Transparency in architecture. I. Title. II. Title: Transparency in architecture.
NA687.K74 2011
724'.7—dc22
2010041996

Printed in Singapore

www.monacellipress.com

10 9 8 7 6 5 4 3 2 1
First edition

Designed by Claudia Brandenburg, Language Arts

Cover: Tom Phifer, Salt Point House; photograph by Scott Frances
Back cover: Morphosis Architects, 41 Cooper Square; photograph by Iwan Baan

Introduction

In his book *Making Movies*, the director Sidney Lumet relates a story about the incomparable cinematic master Akira Kurosawa. After seeing *Ran*, Kurosawa's late-career reworking of *King Lear* (set in sixteenth-century rural Japan), Lumet asked his colleague how he'd come to frame a shot a certain way. Kurosawa replied that if he'd moved the angle a little to the left, he'd have revealed a Sony factory; a bit to the right, and an airport would have appeared. While we can look at a work of art and make assumptions about its underlying vision, the outcome often derives, Lumet observed, at least in part from motives far different from the ones we typically ascribe to a creator.

With some adaptation, the director's point may also be applied to a popular view of architecture. In many minds, the way a building looks is a matter of form-making—that is, an aesthetic choice largely divorced from other considerations. It is for this reason, I think, that designs departing too adventurously from tradition are rejected as expressions of an arrogant creative will: the assumption is that the "architectural" part of architecture has strictly to do with style.

Certainly style plays a part. But in fact many design decisions are about solving one or another sort of problem or meeting a set of objectives; and what may appear to be aesthetic choices are motivated by considerations having to do with a building's function, its location and circumstances, the cultural context or the message it wishes to send, its relationship to the built or natural environment, zoning or community imperatives—a raft of things. If a work of architecture seems, at a glance, incomprehensible, pretentious, or simply unexpected, an understanding of what was required—and how its creator answered those requirements— can be instructive.

One way to arrive at that understanding is to look at a building from a specific perspective. And as the twenty-five projects in this book demonstrate, an especially useful way to think about architecture is by examining the ways in which a structure is or is not transparent. Indeed, physical transparency in design is one of the most comprehensible of concepts because a building is, at root, openings and walls—transparency and opacity in alternation (with degrees of translucency in between). At the same time, the word also implies a thematic component, one especially suited to a historic moment in which "transparency" in government, business, and institutions—processes that are open, honest, legible, and participatory—is prized. (That transparency can also suggest guilelessness, exhibitionism, or a deliberate attempt to deceive—as in, "you're transparently trying to cheat me"—only makes it more interesting.) Thus, an analysis of a building that begins with a study of its transparency can be achieved in a language—architectural and otherwise—that most of us can speak.

The yield of such an approach can be fruitful: though it would be a stretch to say that each of the designs contained herein deals with the subject in an *entirely* different way, what follows is surprisingly prismatic. There are—not surprisingly—projects that deal with view management, privacy versus exposure, and the mitigation or embrace of nature. Yet transparency is also applied to more unexpected tasks, including the facilitation of intimacy within families; the suppressing of undesirable circumstances and the foregrounding of favorable ones; the promotion of a rich interplay between an institution and its surroundings; the encouragement of both the individual and the communal, often simultaneously; the subversion or transformation of an urban condition; the reinforcement of brand identity and workplace amity—considerations, in short, that touch upon every aspect of life.

Two themes emerge as predominant, pertinent to both the moment and the longer term. The first is the relationship between transparency and performance. As the architect Thom Mayne observes, a building's skin has to be "multivalent"—that is to say, capable of doing more than one thing—and many of the projects that follow are clad in ways that enable them to be heated and cooled more efficiently, less expensively, and with a minimum use of non-renewable resources. (And as with race cars whose sleek profiles enhance their aerodynamic efficiency, high-performance buildings can also exhibit high style.)

The second thread running through many of these projects is the balance between the public and private realms. The extent to which the built environment invites the world in or, alternatively, projects its programs out can dramatically influence the ways in which a society chooses to define itself, affecting issues as diverse as the repopulation of cities and the democratic nature of institutions. At every scale, a design's transparency—in every sense of the word—is paramount.

"Reading a building" doesn't come naturally to me, and despite having written about hundreds of projects, at times I still struggle to parse the language of architecture—to transcend the inevitable positive or negative reaction to a form and see beneath a building's skin to its essence. Over and over, a consideration of transparency has enabled me to find my way into even the most resistant designs, consequently transforming the world I inhabit from street after street of structural strangers into a landscape I appreciate, at best, for its variety, originality, and, indeed, maturity. My hope is that *Immaterial World* will help its readers to discover the—entirely transparent—pleasures of doing the same.

Siamese Towers
Santiago, Chile

The form of this structure—a computer building on the campus of the Universidad Católica de Chile—derived from Alejandro Aravena's observation that "no single material should be expected to do everything well." When the university asked Aravena to design an iconic glass tower, he found himself resistant: a strong vertical element among mostly four-story buildings might seem out of place; computer work requires modulated illumination, while a curtain-wall structure would be infused with daylight; and, not least, an uncomfortable greenhouse effect, given the hot Santiago sun, was virtually guaranteed.

Pondering the task, it occurred to Aravena to "split the big problem into smaller ones," he says. "Instead of asking glass to do well from an energy standpoint, let it do what it is good at—resisting dust, pollution, rain. And then put another building inside that is a complement to the exterior—very opaque, good for saving energy and creating darkness—but don't ask this building to do well against dust, pollution, or rain."

Accordingly, Aravena's design sets a rectilinear fiber-cement structure within a floating glass skin. The flared form of the glass, which, like the enclosed volume becomes two-headed at the seventh floor, derives from the changing distance between the two elements, which varies from three meters at ground level (to provide gathering space for students) to ninety centimeters above (just enough room for window washing). While the variation gives the building its suave profile, it also eliminates undesirable solar heat gain. As well, Aravena left a seventy-centimeter space between the curtain wall and the ground, which permits fresh air to enter and heat to be drawn up and expelled through openings at the top—a "vertical wind" naturally accelerated by the narrowing of the skin near the seventh floor. As a result, says the architect, "your first experience isn't visual, it's tactile—the temperature becomes six degrees cooler."

Aravena's architectural replication of conjoined twins "was a response to the client's desire to make a strong statement," he explains. "We didn't have enough square meters to do a really vertical building—if you imagine it without the split you see a very chubby object." The division results in a striking structure—a pair of slender buildings, says Aravena, "that happen to share a big part of their bodies"—with a flexible dualism enhanced by the use of standard aluminum mullions for one side and black-tinted ones for the other. These impart different colors to the glass, a difference that becomes more or less pronounced depending upon the viewpoint. "We wanted to play with the capacity of the building to be one or two," the architect says.

Splitting the problem, which enabled Aravena to use inexpensive fiber-cement and what he calls "the cheapest glass you can buy," resulted in a cost-friendly outcome that resolved all the university's needs. The varying transparency "is a consequence," he admits. "But once you have it, you'd better take advantage of it."

2005
Alejandro Aravena

The angled glass curtain wall of Alejandro Aravena's Siamese Towers encloses a strictly rectilinear fiber-cement building. Narrow windows in the inner structure permit views while minimizing the effects of daylight on computer screens.

14

The glass curtain wall is held in place by structural beams that protrude from the inner building. Varying the lengths of the beams enabled Aravena to change the distance between the glass and concrete elements from three meters at ground level to ninety centimeters above.

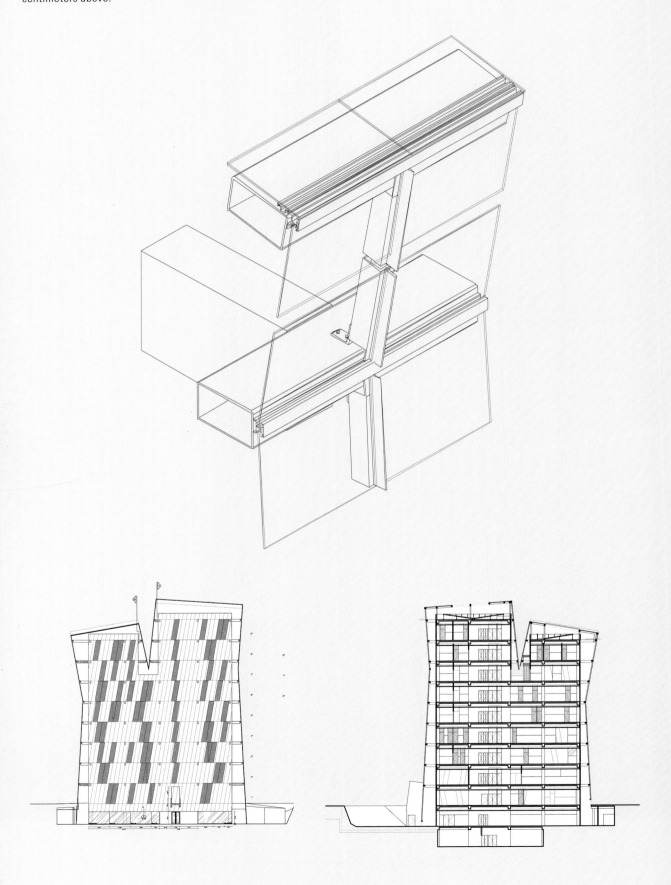

The tower's base, constructed from old railroad ties, "is kind of a huge bench on which to sit—it creates the right place to waste time between classes," says Aravena. The architect achieved the twins' difference in color by using black-tinted aluminum mullions for the glass on one of the towers.

Salt Point House
Salt Point, New York

Thomas Phifer has become known for bravura residential architecture—his 2002
Taghkanic House is often cited as one of the most significant of its decade—but, he
says, "I like doing small things—a simple program, not much money." Phifer got his
wish when a Manhattan-based couple asked him to design what he calls "a contemporary cabin" for a nine-acre property overlooking a pond in New York's Hudson
Valley. "They told me they wanted a house they could use, where they could go
quickly in and out," the architect recalls. "Nothing precious."

Phifer obliged the pair with a 2,200-square-foot two-story structure of the utmost
simplicity: screen porch, living/dining/kitchen zone, and sitting room/stair hall below;
two bedrooms and study upstairs. To capture the "unified, monolithic warmth" that
preserves the unfussy mandate, the entire interior—walls, floors, and ceilings—is
finished in maple plywood. Citing what he describes as "the Japanese and Shaker
practice of highlighting the landscape by framing views," the architect contrasted
the house's fully glazed ends on the first floor with long bands of horizontal side
windows. Upstairs, alternatively, the side walls are solid—"we wanted the sleeping
floor to be more monastic," Phifer explains. Overhead illumination, from two rows
of skylights, remains "quiet, consistent, and simple."

What Phifer calls the house's "heroic" quality—and its elegant replication
of nature—derives from its three moments of verticality. Two of them—the

double-height skylit spaces at each end—are straightforward. The third, however, is a surprise: Phifer set a glass ceiling above the kitchen, at the structure's center, that permits passage of sunlight from two rooftop openings. The architect likens each to those moments when, walking beneath branches in the woods, the leafy canopy abruptly parts and, he says, "opens you to the heavens."

Temperature control inspired the design's defining feature: twin layers of corrugated, custom-perforated steel that float eight inches off the eastern and western facades and—extending above and beyond the structure into softly dissolving, translucent edges—make the house, in its natural setting, seem encased in an industrial chrysalis. "It's a thermal envelope, to absorb the heat of the sun, which then rises up in the cavity behind the skin and leaves," the architect says. Yet the steel's impact remains primarily aesthetic—at once giving the small structure a surprising monumentality and, paradoxically, making it seem to disappear: capturing the shapes and colors of its surroundings; transforming from a hard white solidity to a feathery delicacy as the sun's position changes; seeming to nearly vanish after dark.

"As an architect, you never know exactly if something's going to work," Phifer admits. "But the skin turned out to be beautiful—it gives the house its character."

2007
Thomas Phifer and Partners

The house's twin custom-perforated and -cut corrugated steel facades, which were crafted in Germany, form "an environmental layer that protects the house from radiant heat," explains Thomas Phifer. "It looks beautiful and blends in with the nature all around it."

Paired rows of operable skylights, a dozen in total, work in combination with the structure's porous floor plans and cross-ventilating ends to eliminate the need for air conditioning. The floating stairs leading to the entrance were inspired by Mies van der Rohe.

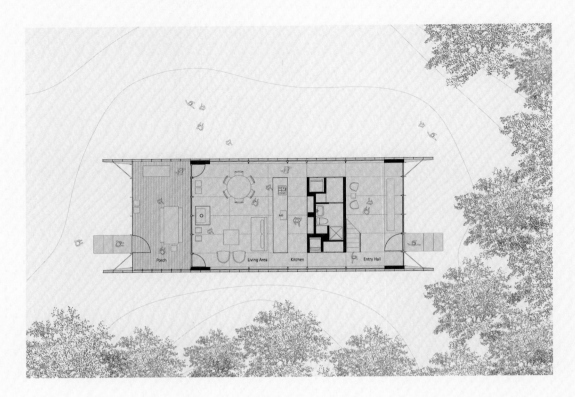

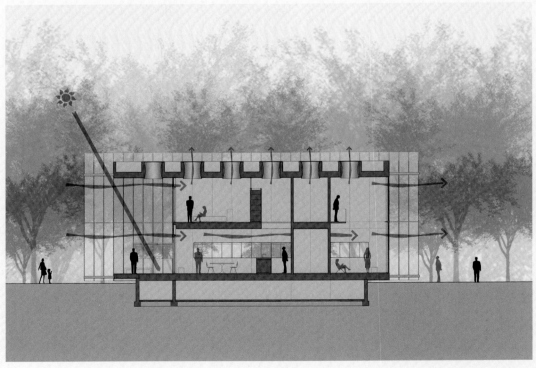

A glass hallway floor, on the second story at the center of the house, allows natural light from two skylights to reach the kitchen below. "I've always admired the Hudson River Valley painters—how monumental their landscapes look," Phifer says. "I wanted this tiny house to have that monumentality."

"The transparency in this house is more framed," Phifer explains. "Side windows frame the views horizontally. And the big windows on the ends frame large views of the landscape and heighten the sense of place." The architect says he "wanted to keep the palette really simple—glass, wood, steel mesh."

Svalbard Science Center
Longyearbyen, Spitzbergen, Svalbard, Norway

"It's one of the most exotic places on the planet," says Einar Jarmund of Longyearbyen. An old Norwegian coal-mining town on an island between the mainland and the North Pole, with a full-time population of about one thousand, Longyearbyen is the northernmost settlement in the world, according to Jarmund, and the site of Jarmund/Vigsnæs's design for the Svalbard Science Center. A university building for research in Arctic studies, the structure extends an existing building from three thousand to twelve thousand square meters and includes educational and administrative facilities, equipment storage, and space for other institutions, notably the Svalbard Museum, which covers the natural and cultural history of the region.

"A special place requires a special structure," Jarmund observes, and his firm, which had previously designed a building for the local governor, understood the challenges posed by the climate. The permanently frozen ground cannot provide the necessary support for a structure. Though snowfall remains moderate, powerful winds blow it back and forth, piling up huge drifts that block doors and windows; since the air is exceptionally dry, the blowing snow becomes as hard and granular as salt and works its way into even the smallest structural joints. And there is the simple fact of the cold, which takes its toll on materials and construction.

The center's slightly menacing appearance, which has been likened to that of a sprawling serpentine monster, evolved in response to these conditions. The aerodynamic angles of the facades, none of which exceed 60 degrees, are the product of computer-generated climate studies and stop snow from piling up around and atop the building. Elevating the structure prevents the permafrost ground cover from melting; cladding the center in metal roofing material enables it to release humidity while keeping out the particles of ceaselessly blowing snow. Jarmund/Vigsnæs encased their earlier building in zinc, which becomes unworkably hard in frigid weather; this time, copper—which grows softer—was selected to permit a longer construction season. For insulation purposes, glazing was kept to a minimum, with small panes reserved for individual work spaces and larger ones for communal areas.

"When you're dealing with a complex program, it's an easy form to work with, because you can stretch the skin if you need more space," says Jarmund. This flexibility is evident in the interior, a series of warm, pine-clad, sculptural zones—corridors with the narrow quality of mine shafts, soaring communal spaces featuring integrated seating—that own the primitive coziness of a cavern. "It's an extremely hostile climate," Jarmund observes. "This makes an interior campus where people can meet."

While the structure was shaped by its surroundings, Jarmund admits, "We like situations where we can have an external reason for doing something that is strange. The beauty of architecture is that it appears when one looks at it—we have no right to insist that the building be understood in a certain way."

2005
Jarmund/Vigsnæs
Architects MNAL

30

The shape of the Svalbard Science Center, located at the convergence point of two valleys in Longyearbyen—which lies north of the Arctic Circle—derived in part from computer-generated snowdrift studies, according to Einar Jarmund. The building's shape prevents snow from piling up.

Jarmund/Vigsnæs clad the building in copper, which becomes soft and easy to work with in extreme cold, to extend the construction season and complete the center quickly. Because glass loses heat "about ten times faster than a well-insulated wall," Jarmund says, large windows were reserved exclusively for public spaces.

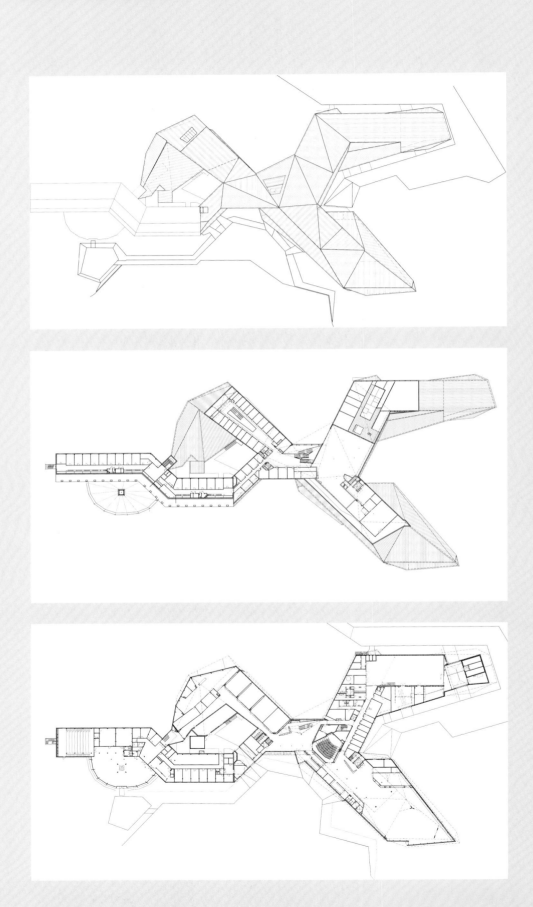

"Since we added onto an existing building, we had very limited ceiling heights—only about ten feet," Jarmund explains. "When we put in the ventilation system, we created a sort of sculptural ceiling to make room for all the ductwork. Then we clad the whole interior in a single material to cope with the acoustical problems you always find in corridors and common areas."

Palms House
Venice, California

"When you're in a multigenerational situation, affording privacy is more important than establishing proximity," says Kevin Daly of a project his firm undertook for a couple with a young child in the western Los Angeles district of Venice. On the serene, secluded property, a main house and a garage with an upstairs guest apartment faced each other across a planted courtyard—an ideal arrangement for the couple and the husband's East Coast–based parents, who were frequently in residence. Apart from renovating the two dilapidated stucco boxes, the challenge, as Daly's epigrammatic observation suggests, lay in enabling the two families to live together without crowding one another actually or psychologically—"establishing openness between the structures, but keeping a certain level of visual separation," the architect says.

Daly Genik's renovation extended the main house, a one-bedroom structure with a mezzanine, approximately six feet into the garden, making room for two bedrooms and baths on the expanded second floor and a small guest room below. The architects also reorganized the guest apartment via the insertion of a freestanding storage unit, incorporating a fireplace that separates the public and sleeping zones. Because Venice real estate remains expensive, the clients, says Daly, "didn't want to sink a whole bunch more money into it," and so the house, apart from its casework, features simple materials and finishes and—thanks to photovoltaic panels on the roof—has "a low energy appetite."

Establishing visual separation proved complex, and after rejecting various structural gambits Daly Genik hit on the idea of partially cladding both structures in angled, perforated-metal panels, pierced by selective view slots, that suggest giant armor helmets. In addition to serving as sunshades, these screen wraps—which also support second-floor balconies that project over the courtyard from both buildings—create layers that make direct visual communication between the structures more difficult. For example, Daly explains, "if you're sitting in the pied-à-terre, there's a layer of glass, then the perforated boundary of the balcony, the big ginger tree in the courtyard, then the perforated metal on the other side, and another layer of glass." What's more, as the landscape is reflected on the panels, and the panels are reflected in the glass—and the panels grow more or less translucent depending on interior and exterior lighting conditions—"the experience of inhabiting the site is complex and ever-changing."

As Daly observes, "Treating the envelope as something that's neither opaque nor transparent is an opportunity to address how exposed we feel, how secure, all the things that go into how you experience a particular space. And what's interesting is that dealing with translucence gives us an opportunity to explore a set of visual characteristics—to look at the ambiguous boundary space that's neither inside nor outside."

2009
Daly Genik Architects

"We considered a lot of different types of skins, including ones that were part of the fabrication process," Kevin Daly recalls. "At one point we designed additions to be built from a plywood grid that was clad with a shrink-wrap material, but it was more construction than we needed to do." Ultimately, the metal mesh screens delivered the requisite level of privacy and proved relatively inexpensive.

"Something interesting about transparency in architecture is that there's an implicit level of performance," Daly observes. "Whether it's shading or allowing a building to be more open than it would have been otherwise, these things end up having specific relationships to a structure's environmental performance."

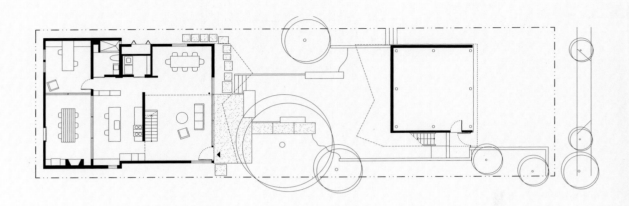

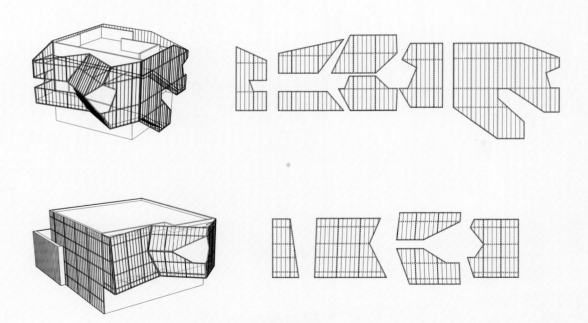

Alice Tully Hall
New York, New York

Lincoln Center, a sixteen-acre complex on Manhattan's Upper West Side, has remained, since the first of its theaters opened in 1962, one of America's premier showcases for the performing arts. Though a richness of cultural institutions benefits every city, the center's development was partly an act of urban renewal. Some seventeen blocks of tenement buildings were demolished (and seven thousand families evicted) to make way for it, and the high-handedness—some would say elitism—with which the life of the neighborhood was erased remains evident in its design. Conceived to be what Elizabeth Diller calls an "urban Acropolis," the core of the campus is a superblock that eliminates several crosstown streets and locates the complex's parking and structural systems underground—thereby raising it, psychologically as well as actually, to a higher elevation. "That was perfect in the eyes of the late '50s planners," Diller explains. "It privileged vehicles over pedestrians and was very much about closing down the grid and keeping out the neighbors."

Perhaps the most problematic of the buildings in this regard was the last to be completed (in 1969): Alice Tully Hall, which also houses the Juilliard School. Sited across the street from the main campus, at the corner of West Sixty-fifth Street and Broadway, Pietro Belluschi's intriguing brutalist structure proved aesthetically divisive—popular with design critics, less so with the public. Its principal shortcomings, however, were urbanistic. The hall was connected to the rest of Lincoln Center by a two-hundred-foot-wide plaza that extended from the second floor of the building southward across West Sixty-fifth, converting the street into a grimy cavern. Moreover, because the original architects set Juilliard's entrance on the plaza level, they were compelled to add a broad second-story exterior walkway that, as it turned the building's corner and terminated in a stair leading down to Broadway, largely concealed the already meager entrance to the concert hall. The triangular street-corner plaza in front of it—the result of placing a rectangular structure on a trapezoid-shaped site—felt as unwelcoming as the building itself.

Engaged to redesign Tully Hall as part of an overall campus revivification, Diller Scofidio + Renfro (with FXFOWLE as associate architect) faced practical considerations—enlarging the lobby and box office, expanding Juilliard by forty-five thousand square feet, upgrading the concert hall. But the larger objective, Diller observes, was "democratizing the site—making good on the 'publicness' of it by infiltrating the city into its spaces."

Diller characterizes the firm's approach as "an architectural striptease." Demolishing the second-floor plaza "was the one big move that changed everything": apart from opening West Sixty-fifth Street to the sky for the first time in forty years, it enabled the architects to create a new and transparent street-level main entrance to Juilliard where previously had been a solid wall beneath an overpass. Eliminating the plaza also allowed Diller Scofidio + Renfro to remove much of the second-floor walkway and stairs that had obscured the concert hall's front doors.

Ungirdled from its exterior circulation elements, Tully was now free to move. Needing, in Diller's words, "to capture more real estate," the architects pulled the rectangular building out toward the trapezoidal lot's line, creating a triangular corner with Juilliard filling the top three floors and the expanded box office and lobby (with a new restaurant) down below. Finally—the striptease's last gyration—the firm sliced away the entire masonry corner of the building beneath the projecting canopy formed by Juilliard's three floors and replaced it with towering glass walls—thereby exposing the concert hall's vast public space entirely to the street.

Unlike those of Lincoln Center's other theaters, Tully Hall's lobby is set below street level, a condition the architects exploited to further increase the building's transparency. Whereas concertgoers once entered a confining box office vestibule before walking downstairs, Diller Scofidio + Renfro set the point of descent well outside near the property line, excavating an expansive plaza that diminishes the difference between the public and private realms. As a result, a formerly desolate corner has become a popular gathering place—a magnetized urban moment that draws in the community and encourages public participation.

"Every architectural opportunity was an urbanistic opportunity," Diller observes. "It's hard to change urban-scale things, but an accumulation of local gestures can produce a very different urban approach." The new Alice Tully Hall is just such a gesture—one that represents its own social moment as strongly as did the original.

2009
Diller Scofidio + Renfro
with FXFOWLE

The three block-length floors housing the Juilliard School (as well as a smaller dance rehearsal space beneath them) overlook Broadway and float above the lobby, restaurant, and box office spaces of Alice Tully Hall. "The biggest complaint of Juilliard's when we started was that they felt very cut off, like they were in a monastery," says Elizabeth Diller. "They wanted to be reconnected to the city."

Diller Scofidio + Renfro drew the southeastern corner of what was originally a rectangular structure outward, toward the corner of the trapezoid-shaped lot. The gesture enabled the firm to at once add square footage to Juilliard above and create a projecting canopy that covers the newly excavated plaza leading to Tully Hall's expanded—and fully glazed—public spaces.

The architects removed a two-hundred-foot-wide plaza that extended from the second floor of Tully Hall across West Sixty-fifth Street to the main campus of Lincoln Center, directly to the south. Doing so opened the street, which had previously felt like a freeway underpass, to the sky and enabled Diller Scofidio + Renfro to glaze what had been a sealed masonry ground-floor facade.

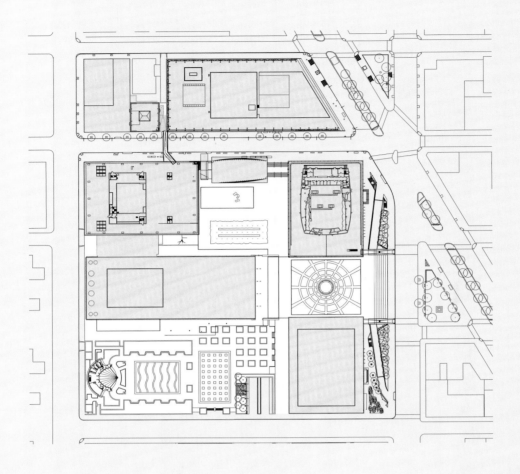

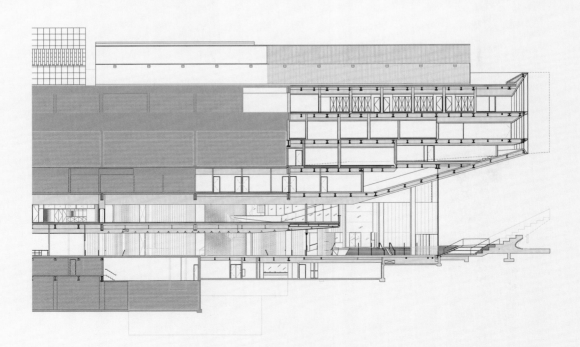

"Everything we did at Lincoln Center came under the umbrella of democratizing the site," says Diller. To open Tully Hall's new atrium-like lobby and restaurant space to the outdoors, the architects replaced the former masonry walls with glass and dramatically elevated the ceiling height. The continuity between the outdoor plaza and lobby helps to erase the distinction between interior and exterior space.

Koby Cottage
Albion, Michigan

James Garrison characterizes Starr Commonwealth, a nonprofit organization head-
quartered in Albion, Michigan, as "a boarding school for troubled teens, from the
inner city as well as more affluent homes, where they can live in the countryside,
do chores and handle responsibilities, and deal with the issues that have come up in
their lives." What the school lacked was a place where visiting parents and children
could spend time together, and so Starr engaged Garrison to create a guesthouse,
on an especially bucolic stretch of land overlooking Montcalm Lake, that might
enable reuniting families to make the best use of their private time and, through its
design, facilitate productive communication.

The architect's thousand-square-foot two-bedroom cottage, set in an X plan
with a dining table at its center, "establishes separate but equal turf," Garrison
explains. "At the remote corners of one of the interlocking axes are the two bedrooms, so the parents and child can retreat when they have to. But as they come
toward each other, they meet in the middle around the table." Apart from the
significance of setting the dinner table—classic locus of family intimacy—at the
cottage's heart, an impossible-to-avoid magnet for the inhabitants, it also enables
the teenager, Garrison points out, to showcase newfound skills. "One of the activi-
ties that allows these kids to get a sense of their abilities is making their own

food," he notes. The table, in close proximity to the open kitchen, "makes the act of eating really central."

While the cottage is mostly composed of small interconnecting spaces, any sense of claustrophobia is mitigated by panoramic views, in particular that of the lake and surrounding woods as seen from the table: the wings widen in a V shape, as though the structure were reaching out to embrace its surroundings. The sense of immateriality is enhanced by the cottage's prefabricated construction: the two factory-produced, steel-clad modules are joined by a linear skylight—the architect refers to it as a "glass zipper"—which makes the entry and dining areas feel more like an open-air waterside picnic ground. Garrison's handling of the design—which encourages family members to face (and face up to) one another, while introducing light, views, and the presence of nature to relieve the pressure—demonstrates a modest yet distinct sensitivity.

"The idea of what constitutes transparency has always fascinated me," Garrison observes. If Koby Cottage's transparency is partly physical, it is also experiential—one that casts openness between individuals as the essence of the architectural narrative.

2009
Garrison Architects

James Garrison's design, with its nearly fully glazed living room and easily accessible roof deck, "gives a couple of people in a thousand square feet a few more spaces to escape to." A main concern was how to keep the cottage both open and closed: "We were trying to allow people to retreat from each other when they had to. At the same time, we wanted to create the potential for coming together."

The Cor-Ten-clad boxes represented "an opportunity for us to implement a new modular technology: a welded factory-produced frame chassis akin to the trellis frame of a Formula One race car," according to Garrison. The south-facing facade of one module, opposite the living room's glass wall in the other module, fills the latter with reflected natural light.

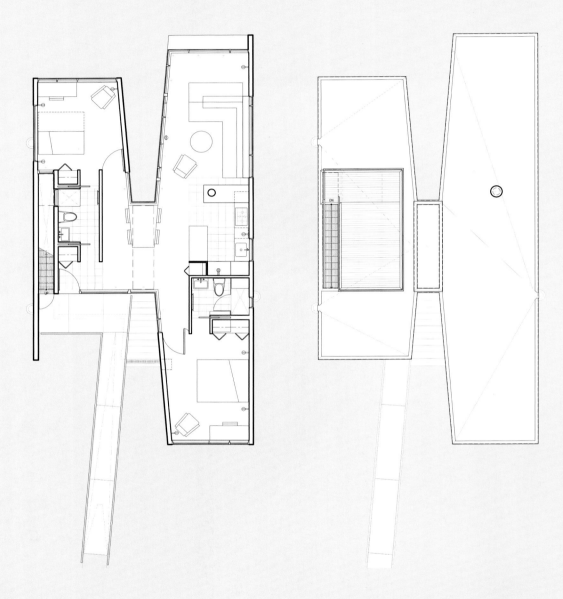

Lauder School of Government, Diplomacy and Strategy and Arison School of Business
Herzliya, Israel

"Light is a terribly important factor in most of the buildings I've done," says Ada Karmi-Melamede—and the home for the combined schools of government and business at the Interdisciplinary Center (IDC) Herzliya, a private college on the site of a former army camp, is no exception. Tasked with fitting the two institutions into a single, heavily programmed building—one that maintained the two-story height of the existing campus architecture—Karmi-Melamede "dug a large hole and put the building in it," setting the first floor of the L-shaped school four meters below grade. Seen from the front—a glazed elevation that faces the campus—the building appears to be two stories tall. The rear facade, conversely, overlooks a sunken court-yard with grand stairways at each end—one connecting to the school, the other to the campus—and reveals its full three-story height. While the government and busi-ness schools occupy different wings, Karmi-Melamede set a circular stack of shared spaces at their junction point. Thus the students from each institution intermingle at the building's dynamic hinge and in the amphitheater-like courtyard with its nearly identical, hangout-friendly pair of stairways.

As felicitous as the design's balance of separate and shared space is Karmi-Melamede's handling of the multiple, and various, opportunities for natural illumina-tion. Indeed, observes the architect, "The light here, which is so intense, is the most important building material in Israel—you can tame it, harness it, reflect it, and when you do it well it brings a building to life."

On the two-story north-facing facade, which receives indirect light, the architect placed "the biggest curtain wall I've made in my life." Karmi-Melamede wanted glazing that would capture the landscaping, "but I didn't want a straightforward reflection," she explains. Accordingly, she alternated transparent and translucent panes of glass, releasing both from their mullions atop the building to create a four-foot-high glazed parapet backlit by the sun—"a much more interesting picture because it's not homogeneous," Karmi-Melamede believes.

On the southern courtyard facade, the architect took the opposite approach, creating a largely opaque composition with narrow side windows on its projecting concrete volumes. The sunken space, with its arcaded line of faculty offices facing the taller, rampartlike main building, abstracts the stone walls and ancient courts excavated in the region's archeological digs.

Karmi-Melamede also introduced an in-between condition along the back of the circular volume, at the junction of the building's wings, using a semicircular skylight some two feet wide and thirty-five feet long. This draws illumination down three stories into the circulation spaces on the first two floors and the third-floor lecture hall. "If I hadn't found a way to illuminate the deepest parts of the center it would have been a dreary space," the architect admits. "Now the light ricochets from one side to the other, and makes the plaster feel like velvet."

2004
Ada Karmi-Melamede
Architects

Behind the large curtain wall, on the school's north facade, is a gently curving, three-story-high circulation corridor that runs the full length of the building and forms an interstitial layer between the outdoors and the school. Ada Karmi-Melamede alternated transparent and translucent panes of glass; "I thought I should do something that shows the garden wants to go inside but can't completely," she says.

Tasked with fitting two institutions into a single heavily programmed building, Karmi-Melamede devised an L-shaped structure; the long piece contains the school of government's classrooms and offices, while the L's short leg houses the business school. The institutions meet at the circular stack of spaces that forms the structure's dynamic hinge.

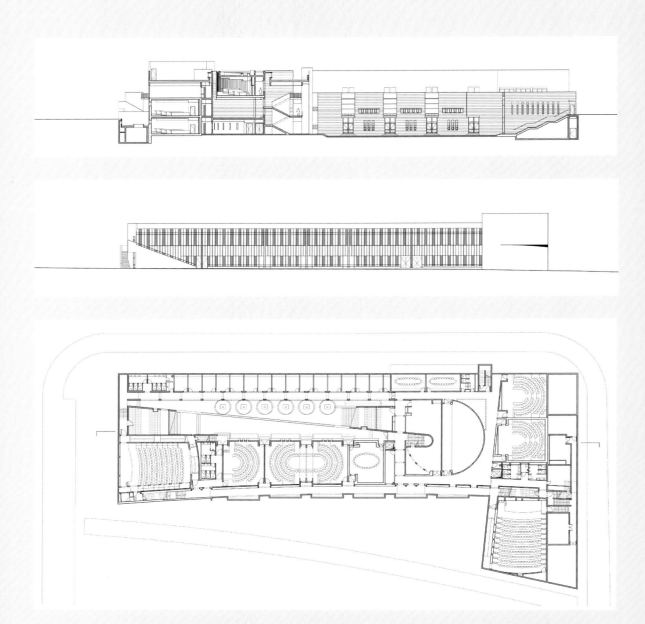

A semicircular skylight, some two feet wide and thirty-five feet long, draws light down three stories along the back of the round volume at the junction of the building's wings, bringing natural illumination into the structure's darkest regions. Karmi-Melamede says the curtain wall is "a very rich wall made with very simple means."

Dow Jones
New York, New York

"The old layout was a warren of workstations and offices—a filing cabinet for people," says STUDIOS Architecture principal Tom Krizmanic of four and a half floors—roughly 270,000 square feet—in the office tower that headquarters Rupert Murdoch's News Corporation. Following its purchase of Dow Jones, News Corp. chose to consolidate that company's divisions—notably the *Wall Street Journal*, Dow Jones Newswires, and MarketWatch.com—in the space; STUDIOS was tasked with creating a design that would enable the print, Internet, and newswire groups to function synergistically.

For Dow Jones, the objective was to marry what Krizmanic calls the "content delivery systems," by bringing the groups' critical players together in a way that facilitates flexible and efficient communication. STUDIOS envisioned this arrangement as part of a democratizing spatial transparency that, says the architect, "creates opportunities for collaboration and gives everybody a greater sense of the whole."

The design expanded the actual and visual vertical connections dramatically, to produce "an ant farm feeling, in which as you walk along the circulation corridors you can see people above and below," Krizmanic explains. In addition to adding stairways to link all the floors, the architects inserted a series of openings that afford multilevel views. (Two LED screens, each spanning several levels, float in the openings and display ever-changing digital montages.) And the corridors themselves, with seating areas for informal meetings, coffee stations with café tables, and white walls that glow with the mutable colors of the LED screens, encourage the social interaction of a public street.

The heart of the office is the "media hub," twenty-eight workstations assembled in a beehive configuration, where the heads of the three organizations and their lieutenants work cheek-by-jowl; because the double-height space is also partly a stage set for periodic live webcasts, video screens display real-time television and Internet feeds, both as reference points for the editors and writers and to create a dynamic visual backdrop.

No less compelling is the project's horizontal openness. Rather than separating the work and circulation zones with solid walls, STUDIOS lightly divided the two with massive panes of blue-tinted glass inserted behind the stairs and multilevel openings. The design also links the north and south sides of each floor by opening up generous corridor space through the massive mechanical core at the building's center. With two-way mirrored and transparent meeting rooms, glass-enclosed executive offices, and most desk space sited along the window walls, the multiple parts of the office are open to one another—and the whole of the space to the city.

STUDIOS's concept of transparency captures the energy of an old-fashioned newsroom. Yet it also expresses the nonlinear, and nonhierarchical, approach to news- and information-gathering made possible by multiple media sources and fluid, rapid-fire methods of content surfing: a dynamic merging of digital, informational, and social transparency.

2009
STUDIOS Architecture

STUDIOS Architecture divided Dow Jones's work and circulation zones with massive panes of translucent blue-tinted glass—a color that, in addition to offering a degree of privacy while still permitting visual connection, infuses the space with narrative vitality by referencing both computer monitors and the "blue screen" backdrop used in video and television production.

In the media hub, says Tom Krizmanic, "you've got the heads of print, of online, and of newswire with their number-one lieutenants right behind them. Out of this, you're getting a faster distribution of knowledge." STUDIOS designed what the architect describes as a "120-degree beehive plan" for the desk, which incorporates twenty-eight workstations. Video screens display real-time television and Internet feeds.

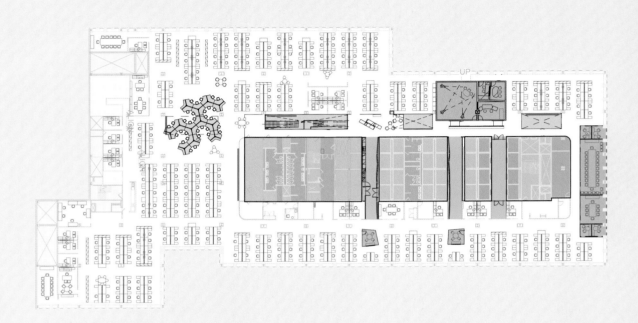

LED screens, each spanning several floors, float in the linked stairway openings and display ever-changing visual montages. Each floor features a circulation corridor STUDIOS dubbed "the main drag," with sitting areas for impromptu meetings and interviews. Two-way mirrored glass makes conference rooms private from without and transparent from within.

California Academy
of Sciences
San Francisco, California

Founded in 1853, the California Academy of Sciences, in San Francisco's Golden Gate Park, owns a number of distinctions. The first scientific institution in the American West, it is also the only one to feature a planetarium and aquarium as well as natural history displays and collections—and one of very few natural science institutions to include facilities for in-house research.

When its complex of eleven buildings, constructed between 1916 and 1976, sustained significant damage in a 1989 earthquake, necessitating partial closure and extensive repairs, the academy chose to rethink its mission in light of modern-day sensibilities. If the natural history museum of yesteryear seemed mostly about dinosaur skeletons and dioramas with stuffed animals (attractions that, admittedly, never go out of style), contemporary thinking about nature is more focused on the health of the planet and the preservation of its habitats and species. Given this change of emphasis, the institution decided that, rather than trying to adapt their existing structures to twenty-first-century considerations, they would build a museum that, while occupying the same site and incorporating elements of the original, could physically embody a contemporary mandate—"a new facility that will not only hold powerful exhibits, but serve as one itself," in the words of Gregory Farrington, the academy's executive director.

Renzo Piano's design, a 410,000-square-foot cross-axial rectangle that brings together new and historic exhibition and research elements around a central piazza, is indeed as much a part of nature as the wonders it displays. This is made manifest by its defining element: a 2.5-acre, partially habitable green roof—carpeted with some 1.7 million native plants and floating at the old museum's height of thirty-six feet—which Piano conceived as a vast swath of the park borne aloft so that the building could be tucked beneath it. Two monumental spherical exhibits—the

Morrison Planetarium and the Rainforests of the World—flank the piazza; with the revivified former entrance to the Steinhart Aquarium, the three serve as the academy's thematic tent poles and, along with four other, smaller hills, push upward to create an undulating surface named, appropriately, the Living Roof.

In addition to insulating the structure and capturing nearly 100 percent of storm-water runoff, the roof's multiple, porthole-like skylights automatically open and close, expelling heat even as the slopes draw cool air into the building, naturally ventilating the exhibition spaces. The aquarium's water tanks capture sunlight from the porous roof, pulling illumination deep into the multiplicitous marine world on the floor below and completing the academy's rich intermingling of land, air, and sea.

Piano also sought to connect the building's interior to its surroundings. "Museums are not usually transparent," he has observed. "They are like a kingdom of darkness and you are trapped inside. But here we are in the middle of a beautiful park; you want to look out and know where you are." Accordingly, the architect created thirty-four-foot-high exhibition spaces with fully glazed exterior walls—specifying an exceptionally clear glass—reinforcing the spaces' immateriality with ultrathin support columns. The piazza at the academy's heart, moreover—with a glass roof, says Piano, "its structure recalling a spiderweb"—permits views to the "hills" above.

"We are excited to collaborate on a project in which design and mission are seamlessly integrated," Piano has said, and the transparency between the two is echoed at every scale: in the exposure of the public to the academy's research facilities and the collaborative, global nature of modern science; in the open display of the building's many sustainable elements; most of all, in the architecture's eloquent expression of the interdependence of all living things.

2008
Renzo Piano
Building Workshop

The largest public LEED Platinum building in the world at the time of its opening, the California Academy of Sciences features environmentally friendly elements at every scale. Among the most notable: a solar canopy fitted with some 60,000 photovoltaic cells that provide approximately 5 percent of the structure's energy needs and prevent the release of more than 400,000 pounds of greenhouse gases each year.

The academy's standout feature is its Living Roof, a 2.5-acre partially habitable greensward carpeted with some 1.7 million plants. According to the academy's botanist, Frank Almeda, "Our goal was to choose native plants that were well adapted to the climate in Golden Gate Park and would provide much-needed habitat for native birds, butterflies, and other beneficial insects."

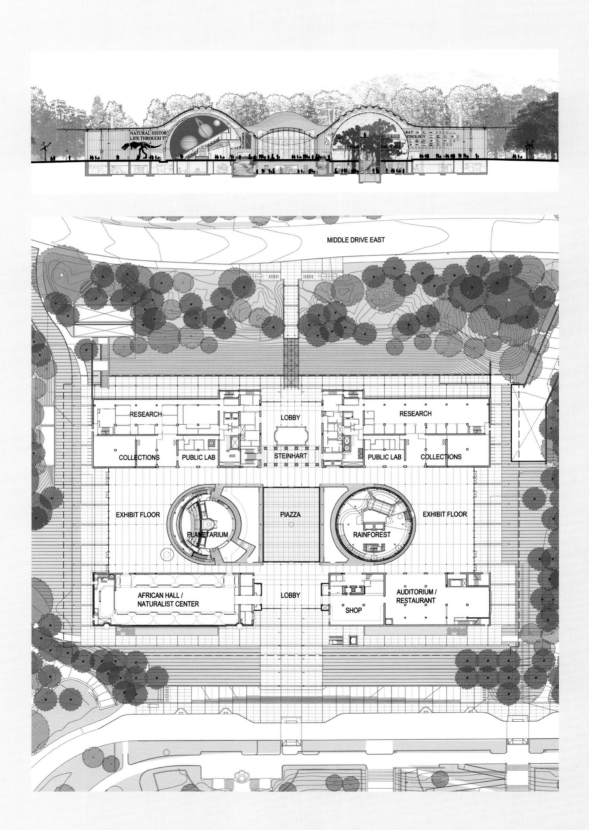

The roof's porthole-like skylights automatically open and close, expelling hot air even as the undulating roof slopes draw cool air into the building through the grand piazza at the academy's center. The glass roof over the piazza has been likened by Renzo Piano to a spider's web.

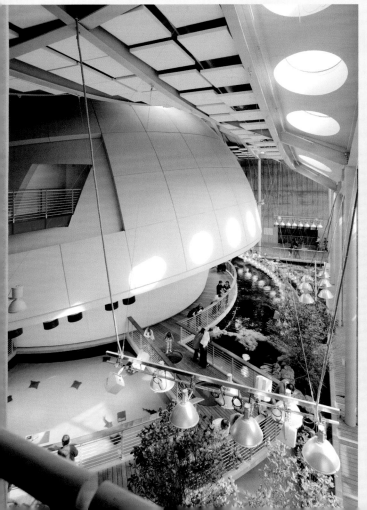

The academy's exhibition halls include two monumental spherical exhibits—the Morrison Planetarium and the Rainforests of the World—as well as a revivified Steinhart Aquarium, which incorporates a two-story swamp and the world's deepest coral reef display. The aquarium features a transparent passageway through its depths and captures sunlight from the portholes in the roof of the rainforest exhibit.

Great (Bamboo) Wall
Beijing, China

In 2002, Zhang Xin—cofounder with her husband Pan Shiyi of SOHO China, the largest commercial real estate company in Asia—embarked on an ambitious act of architectural patronage. Zhang secured eight square kilometers of unspoiled land in the Shuiguan Mountains, near the Badaling section of the Great Wall (some seventy kilometers from Beijing), and invited twelve of Asia's most prominent young architects—among them Tokyo-based Kengo Kuma—to design villas for the site, which they named Commune at the Great Wall. Zhang and Pan "had not been satisfied with the architectural scene in China," Kuma explains, with its "'copied and pasted' buildings from the West." The developer hoped the participants would produce what she characterized as "a contemporary architectural museum," one filled with design-forward work that remained recognizably Asian in character.

For his project, Kuma was attracted to the notion of a structure that, like the Great Wall itself, adapted to the undulant mountain terrain. According to what the architect describes as a twentieth-century model, "you clear the land and build a platform on which the building is constructed. Our thought was to keep the character of the land intact—curve the bottom of the building to fit the ground," thereby integrating it into, rather than isolating it from, its surroundings.

The architect considered bamboo the ideal building material. "It is transparent and opaque, wild and subtle," he explains. "Because of this two-faced character, it merges the binary opposition of outside versus inside, artifice and nature." Bamboo also offered a cultural commentary Kuma found appealing: it remains a traditional symbol of cultural exchange between China and Japan, thereby making the Great (Bamboo) Wall a gesture of unity.

The two-story, six-bedroom villa's bamboo-sheathed long elevations do indeed follow the landscape's contours. But it is Kuma's use of stalks of varying lengths and diameters to lightly divide the interior spaces from one another that infuses the building with a peaceful complexity. This is most evident in a tea room featuring a platform surrounded by a shallow pool and semienclosed on all sides by translucent veils of bamboo that, suspended from structural elements beneath the overhead glazing, hang just above the water. The tea room's placement at the center of the main floor—where it is surrounded by public spaces edged by other bamboo elements of varying degrees of density—gives the villa the experiential richness and pleasurable intrigue of a densely planted forest.

Ironically, despite its appearance, Great (Bamboo) Wall's building blocks remain entirely conventional—even the bamboo is steel-reinforced. Kuma's work is in fact two structures, elegantly combined: a modernist pavilion made of concrete, steel, and glass and a natural enclosure constructed from what is, horticulturally speaking, a grass.

2002
Kengo Kuma & Associates

In his two-story, six-bedroom villa for Commune at the Great Wall in China's Shuiguan Mountains, Kengo Kuma set a semienclosed tea room, surrounded by a shallow pool and translucent veils of bamboo, at the center of the main floor.

Kuma applied "the nature of the Great Wall to the act of dwelling" by adapting the house to the undulant mountain terrain. "This is why the house is called 'wall' instead of 'house.'" The complex of villas of which Kuma's structure is a part was exhibited at the 2002 Venice Biennale, where the entire project received a special prize.

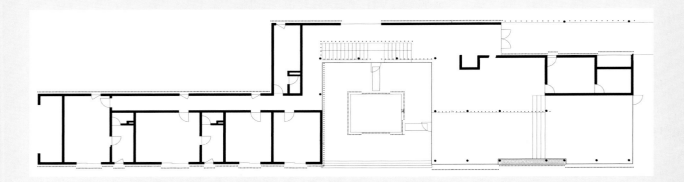

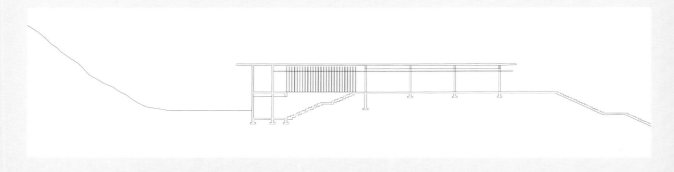

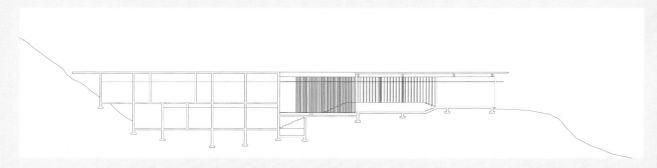

The villa's neighboring public rooms, which adjoin the tea room at the center of the plan, are defined by layers of bamboo of varying degrees of density. The outcome is a designed and constructed interior offering the richness and intrigue of a natural environment.

Renaissance Paris
Arc de Triomphe Hotel
Paris, France

One of the twelve streets projecting outward from Place Charles de Gaulle—at the center of which stands the Arc de Triomphe—Avenue de Wagram is characteristic of the order, imposed by Napoleon III and his urban planner Georges-Eugène Haussmann, that remains the signature (for better and for worse) of Paris. A straight line nearly one mile long, Wagram features masonry buildings, many with flat, aligning facades, that present a stolid, conservative face to the flaneurs strolling its walks. Handsome yet tradition-bound, protected by strict building codes that preserve *le style haussmannien*, the avenue seems almost palpably to resist innovation. How does an architect introduce modernity into such a setting?

That was the question facing Christian de Portzamparc when he was commissioned to create a five-star property, on the site of the old Empire Theater, for the Renaissance hotel brand. His answer—a facade with six floors composed of undulating glass ribbons that, suggests the architect, "seem to form a large interwoven glazed plait"—elegantly explodes the boulevard's monolithic opacity and material uniformity. Moreover, since each of the outward curves forms a floor-to-ceiling "bow window" for a guest room, the design also creates visual and experiential intrigue from both without and within.

"The transparency is more spectacular from inside, because you have the larger view," the architect believes. "The point was to enlarge the sense of the room, to project you into the city and give a 180-degree view" of the panorama extending from the Arc de Triomphe to the Place des Ternes. At the same time, says Portzamparc, "You are in your intimate bubble," a cocoon of privacy enhanced by the lines of ceramic frit that lightly frost the lower part of the glazing, a measure taken to avoid inducing vertigo.

The windows, which facilitate voyeurism not only from the street but from room to room, also inject a faint erotic charge into the circumspect urban setting, initially a concern for the architect. "I thought it could cause a problem," he admits. "But there are curtains, so you can be as private or exposed as you want." And though, when viewed from outside by night, the facade's transparency is dramatic, during the day the highly reflective UV-resistant glazing captures the surrounding buildings so sharply that it can be difficult to peer in.

Portzamparc did not expect the design to be approved by Les Architectes des Bâtiments de France (ABF), the body that oversees the state's protected districts and monuments. By law, buildings within five hundred meters of the Arc de Triomphe must be built from stone. But the official reviewing the hotel accepted it. "He said, 'This is against the rules but it's beautiful, and it is not my duty to be against creation,'" the architect recalls. "It was a good surprise."

2009
Atelier Christian
de Portzamparc

Though the facade of Christian de Portzamparc's design purposely disrupts Avenue de Wagram's historic uniformity, the architect admits to being "unconsciously inspired" by the undulating Art Nouveau facade of the Hotel Ceramic across the street. Portzamparc also inserted a garden beside the hotel with access to the Salle Wagram, a restored Belle Époque–era entertainment hall, at the site's rear.

The highly reflective UV glass, observes Portzamparc, "gives you a baroque vision of the surrounding buildings." The installation of the windows, approximately 2.5 meters high and 3.5 meters wide, "had to be done with great precision for thermal and sound insulation and waterproofing," says the architect, and was complicated by the fact that the undulating panes do not share the same floor plates.

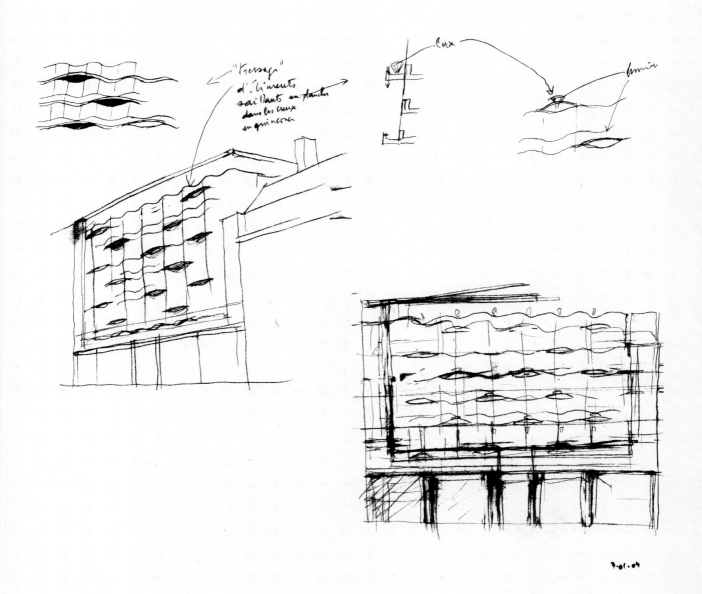

The windows feature lines of ceramic frit, which become more dense at the bottom to create the opacity common in Parisian windows. Portzamparc explains, "In New York, you are more accustomed to seeing the street below your feet, but in Paris it is not so common. This is to give people more of a feeling of security."

Aqua Tower
Chicago, Illinois

One of the frustrations of developing high-rise residential real estate—buildings in which tenants pay a premium for views—is that subsequent construction, especially in dense urban centers, can quickly replace a panoramic vista with a tower full of close-at-hand neighbors. This seemingly insurmountable problem was on Jeanne Gang's mind when she undertook the design of an eighty-two-story condominium/rental/hotel structure north of Chicago's Millennium Park. The high-rise was to be one of nine on a twenty-six-acre site, and Gang recognized that "once the rest of the buildings were filled in, the views would be totally different from what they were at that moment in time."

The architect's solutions derived from the understanding that the project would be constructed from reinforced concrete; since Studio Gang's work, she explains, "is about bringing forward the qualities of a given material, the fluid nature of the concrete was our starting point in thinking about how the building would be made."

Historically, the concrete-slab floors of a high-rise are poured into a form supported by the levels below it. More recently, however, changes in construction technology have produced a "flying form" system that attaches to a building's columns and travels upward more quickly. "On that flying formwork table," Gang explains, "there's a flexible metal edge that could be put into place on each floor in a different way." Because digital design tools make it easier to create varying floor plates with curvilinear edges (as opposed to the usual rectangles), Gang realized that she might design a structure with fluid, ever-changing contours that move in and out to capture ordinarily unattainable vistas—"a vertical landscape, with terraces that bump out and let people see around corners."

Design development began with trying to connect the building to different views. Six major protrusions on the facades were shaped from an initial model Gang describes as "a horizontal topography from which you'd cut out hills, then turned upright." Once they had set the shape, the design team adjusted the curves and cantilevers to provide a greater number of balconies while also crafting places in which they disappear entirely, leaving only exposed glass.

These efforts produced a singular high-rise living experience—in terms of not only outward views but the building's vertical connections, which create an "urban cliff-dweller" effect. Because the terraces flow in and out at different points and to varying degrees, residents can see people above and below them across the facade—impossible when identical balconies are stacked in a line.

The form, which the firm likens to "the limestone outcroppings and geologic forces that shaped the Great Lakes region," has proven notably popular with tour buses. Those hoping to peek in, however, find themselves thwarted. Aqua Tower incorporates six different kinds of glass to answer multiple solar conditions. Where the cantilevers act as sunshades, the glass beneath them is exceptionally clear, providing maximum transparency to those looking out. When the concrete disappears, however, leaving expanses of unprotected glazing, high-performance—and more reflective—panes were used. Thus at precisely the points at which observers might receive an interior view, the surface becomes opaque—reflecting the surrounding structures and sky.

2009
Studio Gang Architects

"When you look at the building from an oblique angle, you really see a lot of concrete, especially if you're standing close to it," says Jeanne Gang of the eighty-two-story tower. "At the same time, we were interested in giving people as clear a view as possible. Because the concrete provides sun shading, we used clearer glass than a typical project, which makes it really transparent for the people inside."

Connecting the apartments to the skyline proved complex, but an even greater brain-twister involved designing what amounted to eighty-two different floors. "You have a balcony on floor twenty-seven in one place, but on thirty-seven it's shifted over," Gang says. "The type and location of the windows and sliding doors, the handrail configurations—everything is unique in every unit."

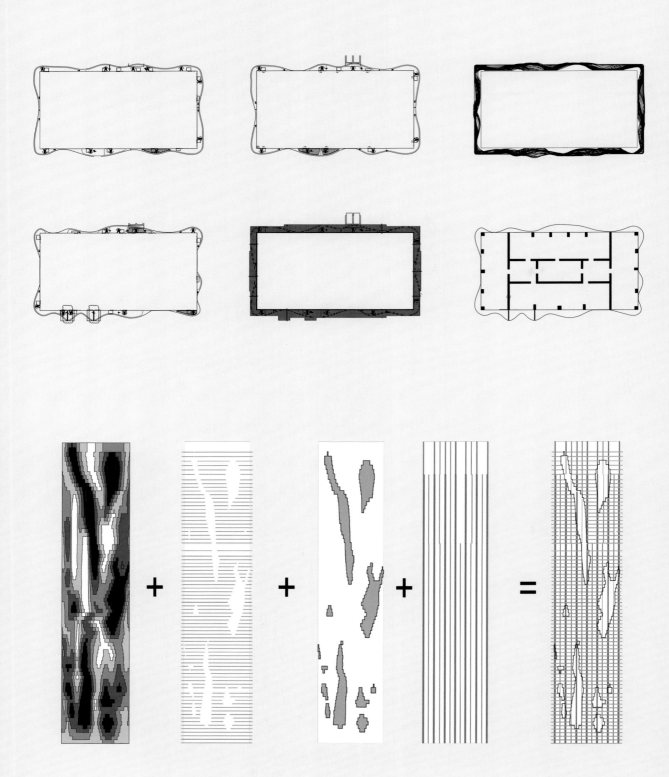

23 Beekman Place
New York, New York

The fate of a work of architecture can be unhappy once it changes hands. Such was nearly the case with the penthouse apartment of architect Paul Rudolph, at 23 Beekman Place in Manhattan. Singularly idiosyncratic, the four-story residence contained some twenty-six different levels and served as an ongoing design laboratory from the late 1970s until Rudolph's death in 1997. Tales tend to focus on the perilous nature of the construction—"it was neither childproof *nor* adultproof," says Andrew Bernheimer—or its drolleries, notably the see-through bathtub suspended above the kitchen. Yet, Rudolph's design was, among other things, an ongoing essay on the nature of space-making and its relationship to perception, in which a deracinating yet instructive interplay between transparency, opacity, and reflectivity remained key. If a visitor did not know precisely whether the space beneath his foot might be a solid or a void, or whether a surface was a wall, a window, or a mirror, the experience—an aggregate of Rudolph's original concept and multiple shoestring design projects built with students—conveyed an excitement about architecture and structure, and expanding the possibilities of both, that remains bracing and inspiring.

After Rudolph's death, the apartment was sold and renovated in the spirit of the original, then sold again to an individual who engaged an architect and got as far as demolishing the interior before inviting Bernheimer and Jared Della Valle to step in. "What was intact was the structure and most of the volumetric relationships," Bernheimer recalls—raw space haunted by the ghost of Rudolph's incomparable design.

The prospect of tackling a classic gave both men pause. The client's program was straightforward: "He liked the idiosyncrasy and spatial arrangements but had some new desires—a gym, a contemporary kitchen, things like that," Della Valle says. But because the original had been forever in flux, adds the architect, "there was no single set of photographs or plans we could look at to re-create it." The task, in effect, involved entering Rudolph's mind and imagining how he might have altered his creation for a client, using contemporary design tools, construction methods, and materials, without banishing its essence.

The architects began by immersing themselves in research "to try and piece together what was there and, more important, to understand what the architectonic language of the place was," Bernheimer says. They compiled "a visual vocabulary of Rudolph's details" and built computer models of the spaces and their components to examine them from every viewpoint.

Thus armed, Della Valle and Bernheimer crafted a thoughtful mix of preservation, interpretation, and invention. Original components were integrated into reconstructed elements. Eighteen-inch-high handrails grew to thirty-six inches yet defined space in the same way. Glass replaced plastic, laminate gave way to Corian, mirror or chrome was chosen over Mylar. New elements became homages to departed ones: the transparent tub went, but the architects replaced it with their own idiosyncratic version that fills from an adjacent overflowing sink.

To create privacy without sacrificing transparency, Della Valle and Bernheimer inserted "soft boundaries" between spaces—translucent two-way mirrors, glass sliding doors, operable layers of fabric. Yet if the apartment has a level of user-friendliness absent in Rudolph's day, it hasn't been defanged: the pair took pains to preserve its moments of instability. "If we'd made the place completely safe, we'd have done it a disservice," Bernheimer relates.

The outcome maintains the scale and complexity of Rudolph's design, its translucency and layering of space, its high-wire edginess and showy glamour. "It's hard to feel like we were authors," Della Valle says. But by demonstrating how historic architecture can be aesthetically and functionally updated without destroying its nature or its importance—in essence, given a new life—the project represents a significant contribution to the conversation about preservation.

2006
Della Valle Bernheimer

"It was renovated upon renovated upon renovated," says Jared Della Valle of architect Paul Rudolph's penthouse apartment in Manhattan. When he and Andrew Bernheimer took on the project, the interior structure and most of the volumetric relationships were intact, but the space was raw.

110

Rudolph attached his apartment to the top of a conventional townhouse building. Though it was nominally a four-story residence, Della Valle and Bernheimer counted some twenty-six different levels, many of them disorienting and perilous to navigate.

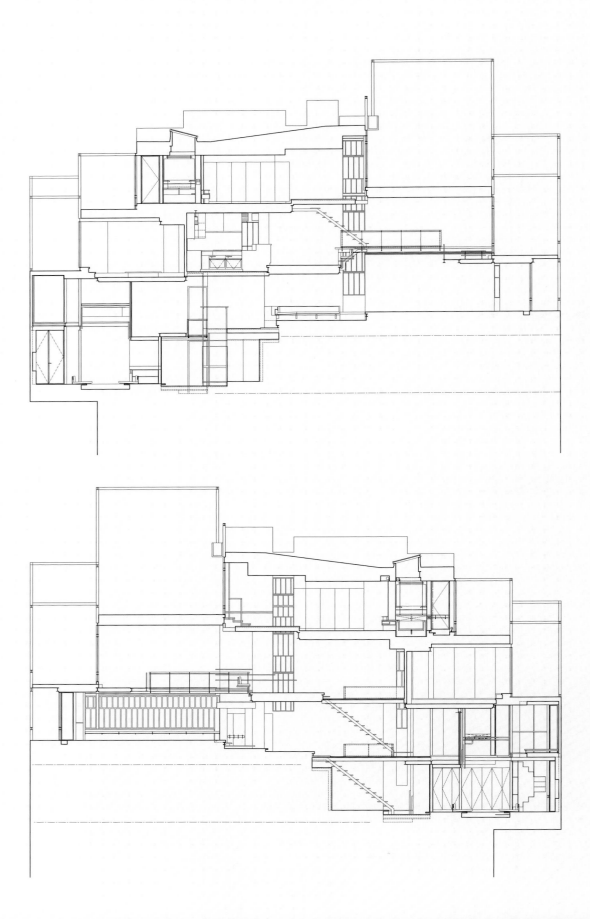

Della Valle Bernheimer's design is an amalgam of preservation, interpretation, and invention. Restored metalwork railings were fitted with new glass panels; glass and acrylic floors were inserted and surfaces were made more reflective to compensate for the loss of a massive window; modern sprinkler and heating/cooling systems were concealed within the structure so as not to compete with the design's drama.

Tietgenkollegiet
Copenhagen, Denmark

One of the challenges of dormitory design is creating a sense of community—one that encourages social interaction and responsibility at every scale—while also giving students the privacy and peace to develop as individuals and, not least, do their work. While many campuses have residential models that support a school's philosophy and objectives—and historic architectural styles to go with them—the need to generate community persists even when a dorm has no specific affiliation, as with Lundgaard & Tranberg's Tietgenkollegiet. The structure, which houses Danish and international students from schools across Copenhagen, was developed by the Nordea Denmark Foundation, a philanthropic organization seeking to create "the future form of student housing"—a mandate complicated by the site in Ørestad North, a developing district that lacks historic Copenhagen's lively street life. Indeed, says project architect Nicolai Richter-Friis, "If you took a garden tool and dragged it down a muddy field, then built along the tracks, it would look like Ørestad—everything is rigid, straight lines."

This rigidity was precisely what the firm wanted to avoid. Instead, Lundgaard & Tranberg developed what amounts to a village in miniature: a structure taking the form of a circle—a "symbol of equality and the communal," according to the firm—that sites 360 bedroom-and-bath units for individual students on the exterior and sets the dorm's communal spaces on an enclosed inner green space.

The outer and inner experiences address the students' personal and collective needs in multiple ways. The out-facing rooms, says Richter-Friis, provide "the city view, and solitude, and you can do your homework and think about stuff." At the same time, a facade of glass, copper alloy, and shutters of American oak individualizes the living spaces—and literalizes the edgy iconoclasm of youth—with varying depths, resulting in what Richter-Friis characterizes as a saw-blade effect. "When you see really slick facades, they can be very precise and beautiful. But this has energy—it reflects that young people, starting their lives, want to flash a bit," he says. "It has more 'ouch,' you know?"

If the facade's shutters convey a sense of discretion and enclosure, the inner ring—with its one- and two-story Lego-like kitchens, common rooms, and terraces thrusting toward the vibrant communal green space, each displaying a different splash of activity—encourages a pleasingly inclusive voyeurism with its transparency. Of this theater-in-the-round experience, which changes as students circle the building's tiers, Richter-Friis observes, "You can stand in your kitchen and find a good party—or maybe that boy or girl you were looking for yesterday."

Tietgenkollegiet also serves an urbanistic function: the form projects its inner exuberance outward into Ørestad North's rectilinear sobriety. Solveig Nielsen, project manager at Copenhagen's Danish Architecture Center, observes, "This round building connects the square ones around it in a special way, and makes a space that's full of intensity."

2006
Lundgaard & Tranberg
Architects

The circular form of Lundgaard & Tranberg's Tietgenkollegiet was partly a response to the somewhat sterile rectilinear quality of Ørestad North, the still-developing Copenhagen district in which it is sited. "Everything is rigid, straight lines," says project architect Nicolai Richter-Friis. "If you took students from the U.S. or Japan and put them in lines like that, like a jail, it would be hard to make them feel part of the community."

Tietgenkollegiet's outer ring is composed of 360 student rooms, their facades finished in copper alloy and American oak, that are set at varying depths and can be privatized and personalized by their occupants. The inner ring, which overlooks a communal green space, is lined with the dormitory's shared spaces, which include laundry, mail, and bicycle rooms, as well as kitchens, terraces, and workshops.

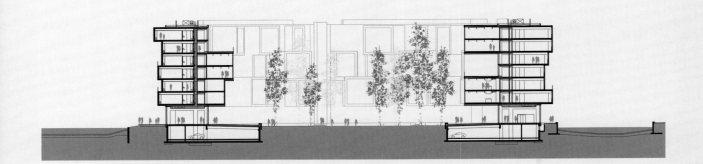

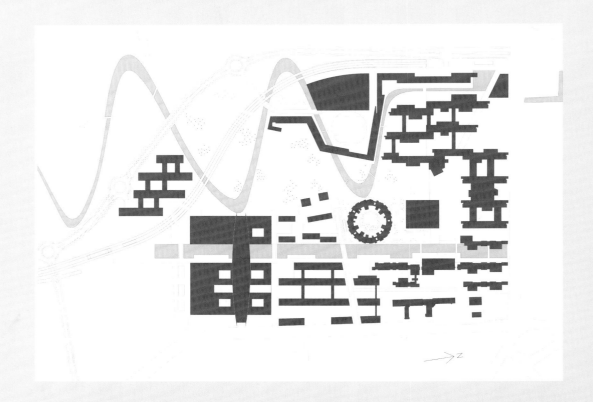

The dormitory's common areas, which overlook one another as well as the enclosed green, encourage a pleasingly inclusive voyeurism that is the essence of student life and forms a counterpoint to the solitude of the individual rooms. "If I'd had a dorm like this, I'd have turned out better," jokes Richter-Friis.

XSmall House
North Cambridge, Massachusetts

Between 2003 and 2006, Beat Schenk and Chaewon Kim, partners in the multi-disciplinary design firm UNI, engaged in an architectural variant of greenmarket-oriented family farming: the pair created a compound of four houses on two adjoining lots in North Cambridge, a mix of design/build renovation and ground-up projects that enabled Schenk and Kim to practice their craft on their own terms, then bring the products to market themselves. After completing Small (also named "Metal Storage"), Medium ("Black Box"), and Large ("Grandma Shed"), UNI chose to squeeze a final element into the limited remaining space, one that would neither spoil the views from the other houses nor violate any of the compound residents' privacy with too-close windows.

XSmall, or "What the Hell is This," lives up to both its appellations. The structure, which more closely resembles a piece of sculpture than a residence—"We wanted to create an object for the other houses to look at," Schenk says—is composed of three nearly identical sixteen-by-twenty-two-by-nine-foot boxes, all finished in broad-grained marine plywood and stacked atop a slightly protruding basement. Though each box has two windows, Schenk and Kim rotated the second- and third-floor elements and installed four skylights per floor—one at each exposed corner—bringing in natural light while maximizing privacy. (A conventional roof-mounted skylight serves the top story.) The house seems hermetic, yet the windows, according to Schenk, "have been placed so you look at something interesting. One side feels more open, and the other—because the building is sitting in the garden—feels more country."

The architects also took pains to individualize each level, finishing the floor of the first in marble, wrapping the second (which holds the living room, study, and a bathroom) in oak plywood, and setting a capacious master suite on top. The experience is surprisingly varied for such a small house, a diversity reinforced by the alternation between the coziness of enclosure and connection to the sky.

UNI built XSmall with exceptional economy (about eighty dollars per square foot), doing much of the labor themselves. On what Schenk describes as a typical working-class street, the house's modesty and material warmth make it a good neighbor to the more conventional surrounding architecture. And, Schenk says with pride, "The skylights leaked the first year, but never again. That's not a bad record."

2006
UNI

XSmall House, which shares a relatively small site with three other UNI-designed residences, is about nine hundred square feet with a three-hundred-square-foot footprint. "If it had too many windows, then people would have privacy issues," says partner Beat Schenk. "So we had the idea to rotate the boxes to make skylights at the corners."

Schenk and partner Chaewon Kim's rotation of the second- and third-floor boxes, all of which are finished in broad-grained marine plywood, enabled them to install four wedge-shaped corner skylights on the first and second floors, as well as two conventional windows per floor. A standard roof-mounted skylight serves the house's top story.

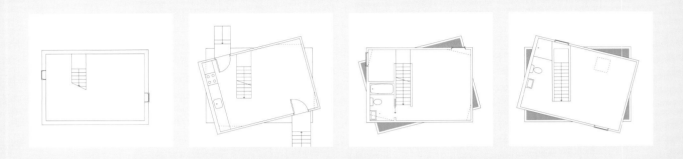

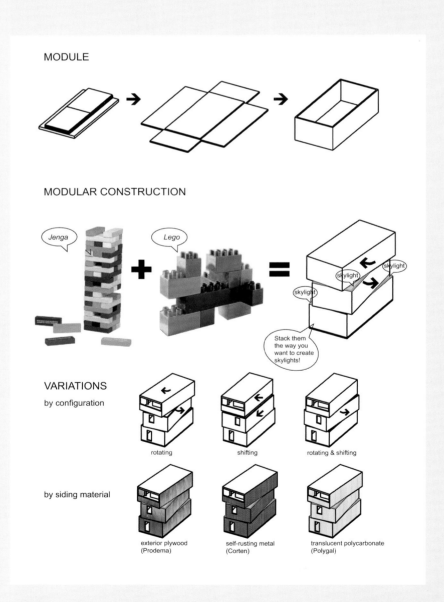

The architects sought to vary the living experience from floor to floor, introducing variety into the extra-small residence. The house, which sits in what amounts to a garden space, serves as a sculptural object for the other three homes on the property and, despite its singular appearance, remains well-suited to the more conventional architecture of the neighborhood.

Tod's Omotesando
Shibuya-ku, Tokyo, Japan

Often described as the Champs-Élysées of Tokyo, Omotesando is a broad boulevard lined on both sides with zelkova trees and chic luxury-brand stores, many designed by world-class architects. When Tod's, the Italian company best known for its driving shoes and handbags, selected Toyo Ito to establish its presence on Omotesando, he envisioned a design that would at once exude the of-the-moment personality of an international fashion label and meet the boulevard's architecturally high bar in a way that might prove more than transitory.

Seeking to differentiate the store from the predominantly glass commercial buildings on the street, Ito chose to express what he describes as "a robust materiality with a concrete structural facade." At the same time, because the L-shaped site forced the bulk of the building to the rear, leaving only a slender, seven-story presence on Omotesando, Ito wanted to give Tod's a "unified volume"—that is, to make it an object rather than a series of walls—prompting him to think of the concrete in terms of its potential as a surface.

Ito envisioned soaring planes that might "escape the conventional notion of a wall structure," which he characterizes as "transparent openings in an opaque volume. Instead of distinguishing transparency from opaqueness, we were seeking a new method that would simultaneously define and unite them," to relate the columns, walls, and openings in an original way.

The architect and his team hit upon the idea of facades that abstracted the signature rows of zelkova trees lining Omotesando—three-hundred-millimeter-thick concrete "trunks" and "branches" interspersed with flush-mounted frameless glass. A tree is a naturally well-engineered, self-supporting organism and "simply needs to withstand its own weight," Ito observes. "Architecture on the other hand needs to transfer live loads and [support] multiple floor slabs. An overlapping network of trees is therefore employed," resulting in an elegant graphic pattern that also delivers the structural bracing ordinarily provided by vertical columns—a system sufficient to support floor slabs of between ten and fifteen meters.

The architect's creation "rejects the obvious distinction between walls and openings, lines and planes, two and three dimensions, transparency and opaqueness," resulting in a building whose aesthetic and tectonic properties are interrelated and mutually supportive—a work that redefines the idea of surface and uses that surface to redefine the idea of structure. It also, Ito believes, serves the brand. "Tod's is well known for natural materials and craftsmanship," he explains. "A concrete tree symbolizes this closeness to nature."

2004
Toyo Ito & Associates, Architects

Toyo Ito's design for Tod's abstracts the zelkova trees that line both sides of Omotesando, a boulevard often described as Tokyo's Champs-Élysées. The overlapping concrete "branches," which become more dense as they approach the top of the seven-story structure, erase the conventional distinctions between windows and walls and give the building what Ito describes as a "unified volume."

134

Ito's design combines thirty-centimeter-thick concrete "trunks" and "branches" with flush-mounted glass—an elegant graphic pattern that also delivers the structural bracing typically provided by load-bearing columns.

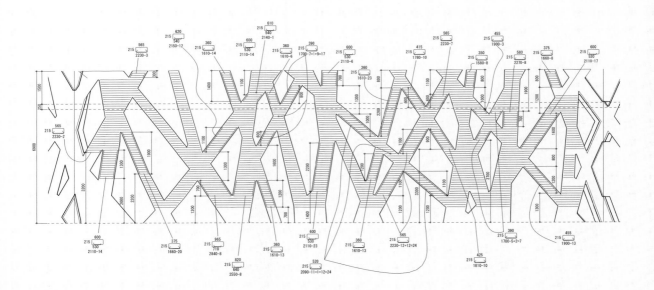

All of the spaces in the building's clear-span floors, each between ten and fifteen meters, have visual access to the concrete and glass facades. Accordingly, the interiors, while discrete, feel as continuous in their character as Tod's exterior.

Greenwich Townhouse
New York, New York

Matthew Baird has long been intrigued by Colin Rowe and Robert Slutzky's essay "Transparency: Literal and Phenomenal," first published in 1963, about the connection between architecture and art. While literal transparency is as it sounds, Rowe and Slutzky's phenomenal variant, Baird explains, "involved the use of overlapping planar elements to imply depth, as in a painting, and how that could play out in architecture."

Baird had a chance to test these ideas when he was asked to design a townhouse in Lower Manhattan's meatpacking district. Though presently the height of chic, says the architect, "when my clients bought, it was still a rough neighborhood, and they wanted something that would feel part of it. I encouraged them to think about the gritty aspect the area had"—its abandoned elevated train line and proximity to the once-mercantile Hudson River piers—"and to come up with a materiality for the house that spoke to that."

Having served as project architect on Tod Williams Billie Tsien Architects' American Folk Art Museum in New York, with its complex multipanel facade, Baird wanted to create "something super simple." He says, "I realized this house is only twenty feet wide and fifty feet tall—surely we can use a single piece of material." Architect and clients considered stone and glass but ultimately made a more unconventional choice: a fourteen-by-forty-foot sheet of plate steel. "I liked the massiveness of it, and the prefab aspect—it could be hoisted off a truck and installed in a day," Baird recalls. The metal, which weathers naturally and is maintenance free, also captures the rough-and-tumble aura of the district's history.

To craft the design's element of phenomenal transparency, Baird installed narrow L-shaped bands of nearly full-height glazing on either side of the steel plate; the architect believes that "these planar expressions imply depth within the shallow thickness of a townhouse facade." Moreover, because the house juxtaposes an opaque front elevation with a completely transparent rear facade, passersby receive a tantalizing peek all the way through the house—"which incites," says Baird, "the human desire to see more."

An unexpectedly evocative moment arose when Baird, who also teaches, took a class to Bethlehem Lukens Plate in Coatesville, Pennsylvania, to observe the steel-making process. Watching a crane pluck recycled materials from different parts of the yard and deposit them in a smelter, says Baird, "I thought, that's so interesting. My facade is made from rail cars, lengths of track, auto bodies"—layers of American life, a narrative variant of phenomenal transparency embedded in the architect's quiet monolith.

2005
Matthew Baird Architects

The front facade of this Greenwich Village townhouse, designed by Matthew Baird, is dominated by a naturally weathering fourteen-by-forty-foot sheet of plate steel, which references the neighborhood's mercantile history and—by bringing to mind the sculpture of Richard Serra—the local artistic legacy. The rear facade, conversely, is fully glazed—and, on the main floor, can be opened completely to a back terrace.

To make the house, with its restricted eight-hundred-square-foot floor plates, feel more voluminous, the architect set floor-to-ceiling glass at every stair landing: the residents are always ascending toward the sky. Nearly half the roof is consumed by a skylight that sends illumination deep into the structure through expanded stairwell openings. Clear panes in place of balustrades afford elongated vertical views.

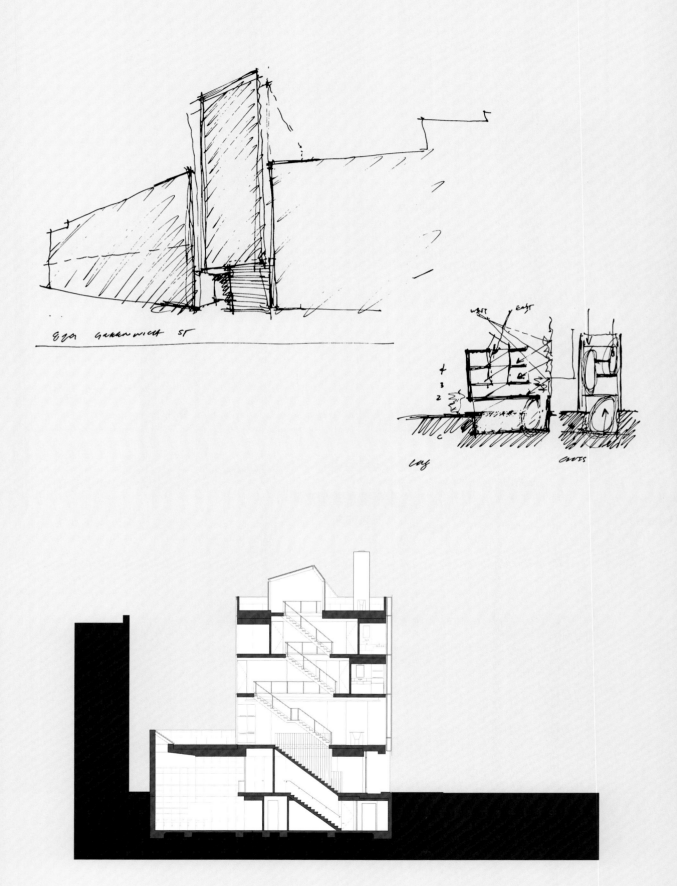

Fiera Milano
Milan, Italy

"I always have two ways to work: A and B," says Massimiliano Fuksas. "A is a very geometric building, and B is very dramatic. I don't like chaos alone. I like to have a simple, regular element to better understand the chaos." The architect's method served him dramatically when his studio undertook the design of the Fiera Milano: at once that most chaotic of architectural typologies, the trade fair hall, and at 2.1 million square feet, one of the largest structures in Europe—virtually a city unto itself. Apart from time and budgetary constraints, Fuksas faced the enduring challenge of trade hall design: creating order out of what is typically a vast and sprawling state of confusion in which participants wander interminably in search not only of exhibitions but of food, drink, restrooms, recognizable landmarks, and one another.

Fuksas was awarded the project on the strength of his organizing strategy: a mile-long bilevel central axis that runs the full length of the fair and serves as its de facto Main Street. While such a straight line might be seen, in the architect's formulation, as an A strategy, he topped it with a stunning expression of B: a continuous, undulating glass-and-steel roof structure, nicknamed *la vela* (the sail), and described by Fuksas as having the qualities of a tornado—swirling down to the ground in places to form kinetic funnels—and expressing the profile of the nearby Alps. Though largely supported by delicate steel columns with branches incorporating drainage elements, the canopy, says Fuksas, plays with the buildings and structural elements along the axis: hovering above some, reaching for others, in a fluid progression that provides shelter, exposes typically enclosed spaces to the sky, shapes an ever-changing prismatic display of natural light, and turns a simple circulation spine into a beautiful, notably human, public gathering place.

Its evocative properties notwithstanding, the axis also succeeds functionally—enabling visitors to contend with the multiple destinations in a comprehensible manner—and Fuksas reinforced this by making the ground floor a for-pay access route to the trade halls and the seven-meter-high walkway a free public promenade. Legibility is also conferred by the differing architectural styles in which the four different types of structures are dressed: the eight massive trade halls are industrial steel-clad boxes ("with a lot of toilets," the architect affirms); food and beverage venues, meeting halls, and offices each have their own visual identity, ranging from strongly rectilinear transparent boxes to opaque metal pods perched on rough-hewn stilts. All of it, beneath the diamond-patterned glazing, remains infused by light.

"It's a nice way to give a sense of happiness and serenity," Fuksas observes. "There is no aggression there"—an interesting trick for a trade fair.

2005
Massimiliano Fuksas
Architetto

The mile-long glass canopy that covers the Fiera Milano's two-level central circulation axis is formed from a steel-mesh structure into which Massimiliano Fuksas inserted triangular panes of glass. "It's a street," says Fuksas, "and you have to have the sky above the street."

After the building was completed, Fuksas realized that the airport had been his unconscious design model. "When I started work on a new terminal in Shenzhen, I discovered it was the same project—Milan has two levels, like for arrival and departure; things are numbered like gates," he says. "When you think about it, the matrix of all contemporary life is the airport."

Fuksas developed the design of the glass canopy by alternating between physical models and Rhinoceros three-dimensional modeling software. "I started with a model, and then I checked it with the guy who was working with Rhino, and he said, 'Here you go a little bit down, there a little bit up,'" Fuksas says. "I go back and forth always between physical models and software."

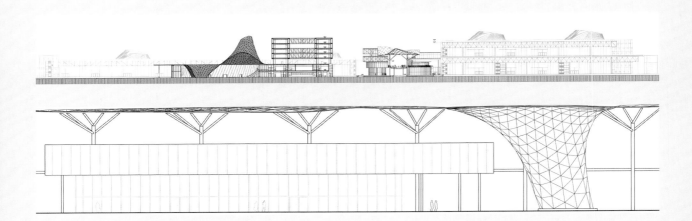

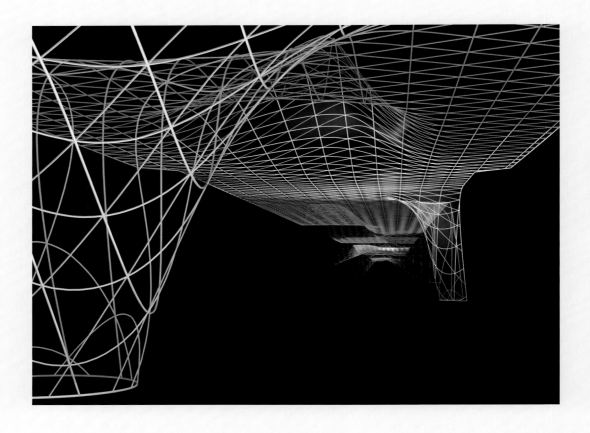

Hotel Aire de Bardenas
Tudela, Navarre, Spain

"What are we going to do here?" Mónica Rivera recalls asking partner Emiliano López when they first visited the site of Hotel Aire de Bardenas, outside Tudela in the Navarre region of Spain. The location was spectacular: within the limits of the semidesert landscape of Bardenas Reales, a natural park and UNESCO biosphere reserve, and near the lush cultivated fields and orchards along the Ebro River. Yet, Rivera remembers, "It was completely flat, no physical references. And harsh—the temperatures are very extreme, and the constant winds are crazy." The clients, however, wanted to take advantage of the government's drive to increase regional tourism, one that came with financial support for developers of high-end properties—which is how Rivera and López found themselves standing in a hot, windy wheat field, pondering the future form of a four-star hotel.

Matters were further complicated by the tight schedule and the fact that one of the clients, with limited construction experience, planned to serve as contractor. "The strategy was, how can we design something simple, economical, and that can be assembled very fast—by someone who does not know how to read a plan," Rivera says.

The architects' design derived from their attraction to the landscape and also answered the project's practical considerations. "Coming from the city, it was very beautiful—the crops are right in front of the hotel, and people are there harvesting," Rivera explains. "We wanted not to take away from this simplicity." The hotel's form—a series of monochrome cubes, loosely dispersed around a central court—conjures up both the shed construction of the area's agricultural cooperatives and, believes the architect, "a wagon train that's stopped for the night and arranged itself into a circle before passing on." At the same time, the structures could be built from low-cost, speedily assembled panels made from sheet-metal-and-foam insulation sandwiches.

The hotel's guest rooms—ten with private patios attached to the main building, the rest encased in freestanding pavilions—incorporate a feature that forms Aire de Bardenas's sole distinguishing element: 2-by-1.5-meter projecting windows that form habitable spaces from which to contemplate the landscape. These meet quotidian needs: serving as children's beds, answering the four-star-hotel requirement for an in-room armchair "without having the usual four-star chair," and connecting guests to the environment while protecting them from it. But they also vitalize the design: inserting a startlingly human element into an otherwise anonymous scheme and converting the sheds into a multiscreen panoramic cinema that reflects the environment—a pristine conflation of the natural and human, intimate and grand.

López and Rivera also benefited from river stones excavated from a nearby construction site, which they scattered in front of the pavilion windows. Because they're difficult to traverse, the stones form a "horizontal fence" that prevents people from approaching the windows. "Except for visiting architects," Rivera admits. "Architects want to see everything."

2007
Emiliano López Mónica
Rivera Architects

Hotel Aire de Bardenas's freestanding guest pavilions, accessed via walkway, are distinguished by oversized picture windows that project outward from the simple metal-clad sheds. Stones excavated from a nearby construction site protect the privacy of guests by discouraging people from approaching the windows. "Sheep can't even walk on them—only dogs," says architect Mónica Rivera.

Needing to surround the hotel grounds with a windbreak, the architects considered hedges (too much maintenance) and boulders ("an architectural cliché," says Rivera) before settling on old packing crates found at a local agricultural co-op. "Our client bought a huge pile of them for nothing," says Rivera. "They're very stable; they work perfectly and look great."

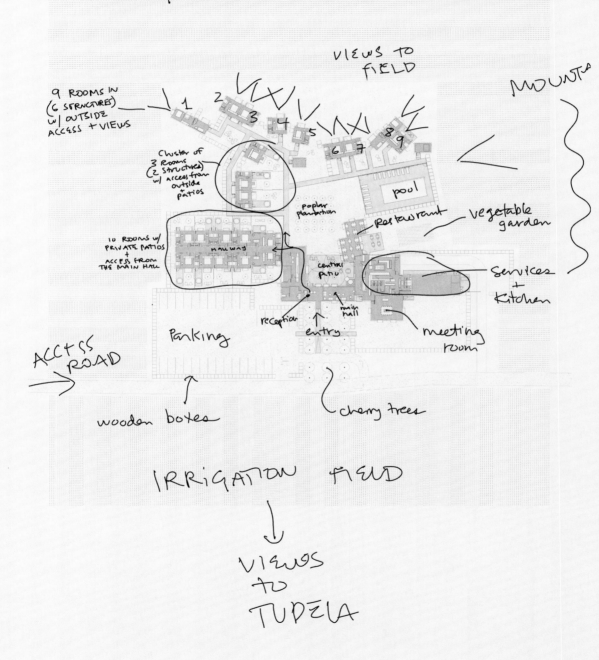

WHEAT FIELD + THE BARDENAS

VIEWS TO FIELD

MOUNTS

9 ROOMS IN (6 STRUCTURES) w/ OUTSIDE ACCESS + VIEWS

Cluster of 3 Rooms (2 Structures) w/ access from outside patios

poplar plantation

pool

Restaurant

vegetable garden

10 ROOMS w/ PRIVATE PATIOS + ACCESS FROM THE MAIN HALL

HALLWAY

central patio

Services + Kitchen

reception

main hall

entry

meeting room

ACCESS ROAD

Parking

wooden boxes

cherry trees

IRRIGATION FIELD

VIEWS TO TUDELA

"You have constant winds, which are very strong," says Rivera. "So instead of thinking of a hotel in the country where you can open the windows and go to the terrace, it's the opposite—you have these windows, which are like capsules where you're absolutely protected." Some feature benches; others serve as single beds. "Kids love them—the first thing they do is go to the window and say, 'This is mine.'"

The highly reflective windows convert the anonymous structures—built from sheet-metal sandwich panels that recall the shed construction of the region's agricultural cooperatives—into a multiscreen panorama that captures the rugged beauty of the hotel's surroundings. "There was the intention of abstraction," Rivera says.

Formosa 1140
West Hollywood, California

The design of this four-story, eleven-unit residential structure was influenced not by programmatic considerations but by Los Angeles's unfortunate distinction as "the most park-impoverished major city in America," in journalist Matthew Fleischer's formulation. "Internal courtyards drive a lot of the building here," explains Lorcan O'Herlihy. "We felt, with so little public space, why not give that normally enclosed area to the community?" O'Herlihy proposed to the developer, Richard Loring, that 4,600 square feet—roughly a third of the property—be converted into a pocket park; the pair worked out an arrangement that enabled West Hollywood to both invest in the project and lease the land for public use.

This act of altruism produced benefits and challenges. Eliminating the courtyard enabled O'Herlihy to create cross-ventilated floor-through duplex apartments that enjoy pleasurable green views and abundant southern light. Yet orienting the building toward the park required a nuanced mediation between the public and private realms—not merely to protect residents from unwanted intrusiveness but to develop a design model that encouraged reurbanization. "As much as people have begun to embrace the idea of pulling away from the suburbs and moving to walkable urban areas, they still want their privacy," O'Herlihy notes. Contributing to a more sustainable Los Angeles required the architect to devise a boundary that let the city in while keeping at bay the things that drove people away in the first place.

The solution—sheathing the structure in a complex choreography of solid- and perforated-metal panels, interspersed with voids and painted a vivid orange and red (a nod to a neighborhood icon, the Formosa Café)—moves between degrees of transparency and opacity to produce a fine-grained variety of public/private interrelationships. Exposed and projecting second-floor balconies establish direct connections with the park and its users. On the third level, O'Herlihy sited an exterior circulation catwalk between the outer wall of the building and its metal skin, leading to the doors to the upstairs units; this semienclosed space enables varying degrees of connection between the apartments, the public space of the building, and the park, but also establishes a common area for residents to casually congregate. The experiential yield is abundant: complete privacy within the apartments; communication between apartments and catwalk; the social space of the catwalk; public/private connections between the building and the park; and the park itself. "The outer skin also keeps the building cool," the architect adds—offering an unintended double entendre.

"You can become more involved in the process of how cities grow, as opposed to just being an architect who's given a program," O'Herlihy observes. He considers this essential. "People are moving into areas like West Hollywood—and they'll leave if they don't get some of what they wanted in the suburbs, which is green space."

2008
Lorcan O'Herlihy Architects

Lorcan O'Herlihy sheathed his four-story, eleven-unit West Hollywood residential building in a mixture of solid and perforated metal panels interspersed with voids that reveal terraces, a circulation catwalk, windows, and the black-painted wall of the actual structure. The panels mediate between the private spaces of the apartments and the public park—devised by O'Herlihy and developer Richard Loring—it overlooks.

"As Los Angeles grows and people embrace the idea of moving away from suburbs and going to more urban areas, as much as they want to be around people and walk to the coffee shop, they still want their privacy," O'Herlihy notes. "How do you address the boundary between public and private space in a way that is interesting?"

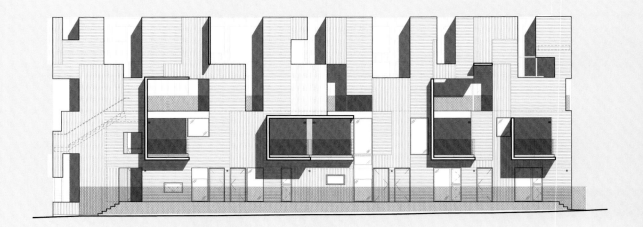

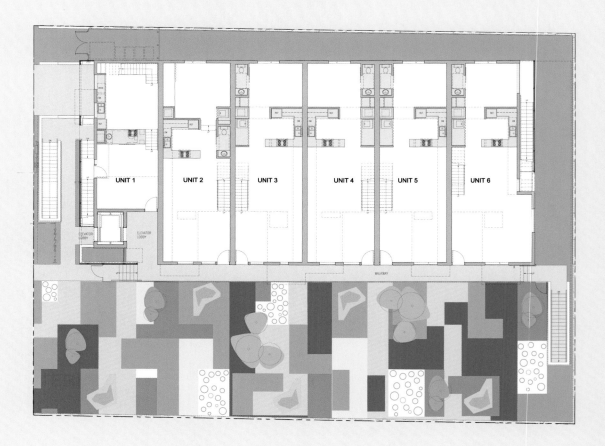

"Only four percent of Los Angeles is [public] green space—one of the smallest figures in the United States," says O'Herlihy. In compensation, the architect and developer worked with the city of West Hollywood to convert what ordinarily would have been the building's courtyard space into a park. "Los Angeles is about public land, not private space—this is the reverse of that."

Yas Hotel
Abu Dhabi, United Arab Emirates

"When we came on board, the sand was just being poured," says Asymptote's Hani Rashid of Yas Island, a twenty-five-square-kilometer fantasyland near the city of Abu Dhabi. Along with golf courses, marinas, theme and water parks, and other attractions (some built, others on the way), Yas is home to the Formula 1 Abu Dhabi Grand Prix; joining the F1 racing season required that the emirate provide state-of-the-art facilities, including a five-star hotel. Accordingly, Rashid and partner Lise Anne Couture set out to "do something spectacular."

The pair produced two twelve-story volumes—one of which appears to float in the marina, the other tucked within the race circuit—enveloped by a fluid, 217-meter glass-and-steel "grid shell" and linked by a bridge that crosses directly above the course. "The inspiration was Monte Carlo, that whole history of driving between buildings and being able to dock your boat and watch from the water," Rashid says. Yet the hotel's sheer dynamism, which seems shot through with the essence of racing, also derives from Asymptote's interest in "making forms that say something about the period we live in. Speed is a hallmark of the age—of transfer, movement from city to city, of information."

Another influence proved to be the region itself. "We looked at the attire—the *dishdashas* and burqas, the fact that people veil themselves for privacy or being in the heat," says Rashid. Also critical was the notion of seeing but not being seen, embodied by the *mashrabiya*—sophisticated latticework window screens—prevalent in Arabic architecture. "It's a hotel, so there's a need for privacy and enclosure, as well as aeration and views of the spectacle of the race," he observes. "That worked with the mathematics of Islamic architecture and Arabesque patterning to produce a veil—the 'grid shell'—over the entire building."

Asymptote's veil is, of course, leading-edge: a steel frame incorporating some 5,680 diamond shapes, ranging in size from .75 to 4.5 meters, all fitted with glass panels. While the sun animates it by day, lighting effects play across the surface after dark: each of the diamonds is equipped with a fixture that turns it into a pixel in what is, in effect, the world's largest video display.

The design, observes Rashid, "is like me—a mix-up: British mother, Egyptian father, brought up in Europe and Canada, schooled in the United States. On the one hand, there's an interest in a highly contemporary way of making things. Other moments represent my memory of the first years of my life in Egypt, of sun coming through the trelliswork. It's a matter of getting the best of those various cultural aspects, and this building has a lot of that."

2009
Asymptote Architecture

The Yas Hotel's two 12-story volumes are enveloped by a 217-meter "grid shell" that incorporates some 5,680 glass panels in a steel frame that seems to have been flung over the structures like a veil. The hotel's buildings are also united by a bridge that crosses directly above Abu Dhabi's Formula 1 Grand Prix race course. Asymptote's design captures the essence of speed.

The diamond shapes of the "grid shell" range in size from .75 to 4.5 meters; they are fitted with glass panels of ten different sizes. Initially Rashid and partner Lise Anne Couture hoped to attach motors to each panel that would permit individual adjustment and even connect to sensors in the track so that the glass would rotate according to the speed of the cars. The cost of the mechanisms proved prohibitive, however.

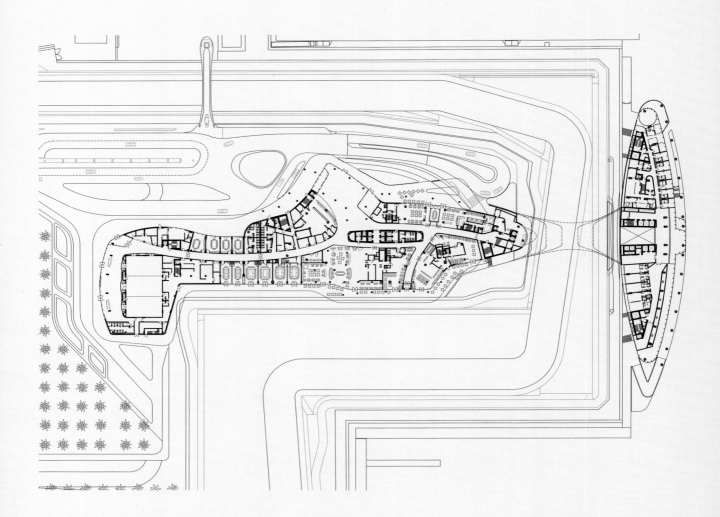

The design of the "grid shell," as well as multiple elements of the hotel's interior, were influenced by Islamic architecture and what Rashid describes as "the intricacies and mathematics of Arabesque patterning." Each of the diamond shapes of the steel grid is equipped with a lighting fixture; working with Arup Lighting, Asymptote custom-crafted scripts for moving images, which are sent out across the entire surface.

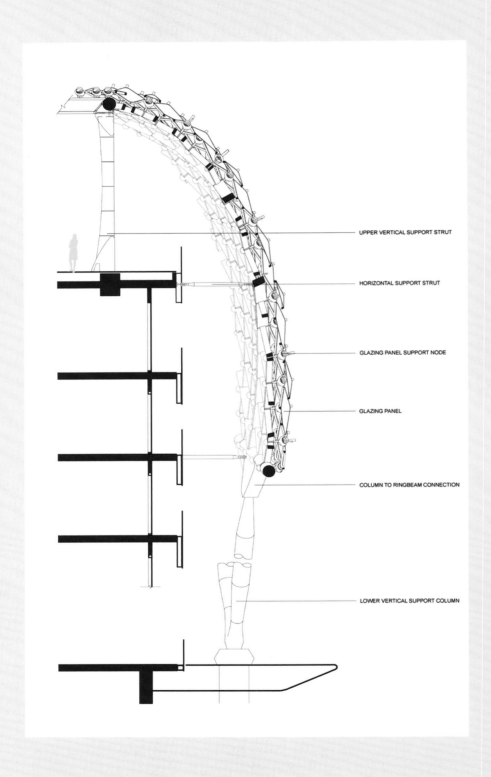

UPPER VERTICAL SUPPORT STRUT

HORIZONTAL SUPPORT STRUT

GLAZING PANEL SUPPORT NODE

GLAZING PANEL

COLUMN TO RINGBEAM CONNECTION

LOWER VERTICAL SUPPORT COLUMN

"On the roof, when we put a certain deep amber light into the 'grid shell,' it color-shifts the real sky so that anything you look at becomes lime green," says Rashid. "My mother was on the roof, and she said she had to see an eye doctor because a bright green plane had flown by above her."

Airspace Tokyo
Tokyo, Japan

"I'm always looking for problems I can turn into opportunities—either functional conundrums or simple desires," explains Thom Faulders. Such an opportunity arose when the Japanese firm Studio M invited the California-based architect to design a screened covering for a new structure in Tokyo's Kitamagome Ota-ku district. The four-story corner-lot building, which houses four residential duplex lofts atop a pair of photography studios, replaced a 1940s residence that had been—atypically, for the densely packed neighborhood of narrow lots—almost entirely obscured by lush vegetation. Faulders became intrigued by the green buffer zone that had shielded the original residence from the street. "That kind of amazing layered threshold seemed an impressive thing to aim for," he says.

For his design correlative, the architect considered the ways in which a canopy of branches filters light and views without eliminating them, and wicks away rain despite being porous. "That breaking up of the elements was what we wanted," Faulders explains, especially because the facades to be veiled featured exposed circulation catwalks and balconies and full-height, voyeur-friendly windows. The result—two layers of screening, separated by a narrow air space (hence the name), that together resemble an enormous monochrome Jackson Pollock painting rendered in three dimensions—protects the outdoor spaces from the weather and offers privacy to residents while enabling them to observe the street.

The double layer was key: the previous residence claimed roughly five meters of foliage between the building and street, whereas Faulders had only twenty centimeters in which to achieve a comparable condition. To capture the requisite complexity, the architect (working with the design firm Proces2) used computer software to create four separate patterns composed of irregular shapes connected by weblike arms. Faulders then merged them into a pair of screen designs—each combining two patterns—and overlaid them, clustering the forms densely over points on the facades requiring privacy and loosely in places where exposure proved desirable.

With the designs finalized, the screens were cut from one-by-two-meter panels of composite metal-and-plastic material typically used as billboard backing; these were bolted to a system of thin, near-invisible stainless-steel rods strung between supports at the top and bottom of the facades, then fastened to one another with rigid tape to produce a seamless impression. "The structure disappears, and the planes seem to float," Faulders says.

The effect, he observes, "is atmospheric. When you're inside, you feel wrapped but not sealed off. As you walk past it, your parallax view is always changing. During the day, the screen is white and the building recedes. At night, lit from within, the screen recedes and the building's expressed—it glows like a lantern." Though his intention was not to mimic the previous residence, Faulders's creation, amid the "beautifully controlled chaos" of Tokyo, achieves a comparable effect. "What we've put up is an anomaly, but like the earlier landscape, it creates an ease—a neighborhood presence."

2007
Building Design:
Studio M
Screen Facade Design:
Faulders Studio

"I was commissioned to design a building wrap that would be the interface between the urban environment and the inside spaces," recalls Thom Faulders. "I started off with a single-layer screen—something more straightforward. But I was interested in replicating the buffer zone of vegetation that had wrapped the previous building on the site."

Faulders used computer software to create four separate patterns, which he merged into a pair of screen designs. He then overlaid the two, separating them with a space of twenty centimeters. "You get a sense of depth that's really quite amazing," Faulders says. From within, the interplay of patterns "creates a whole bunch of variable nuances" as the exterior light conditions change, according to the architect.

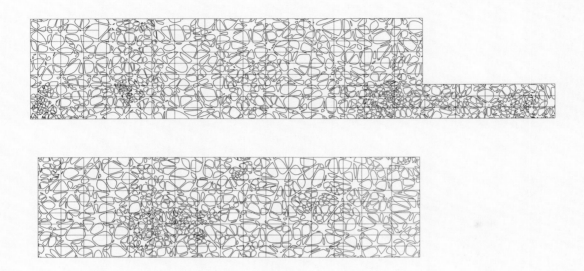

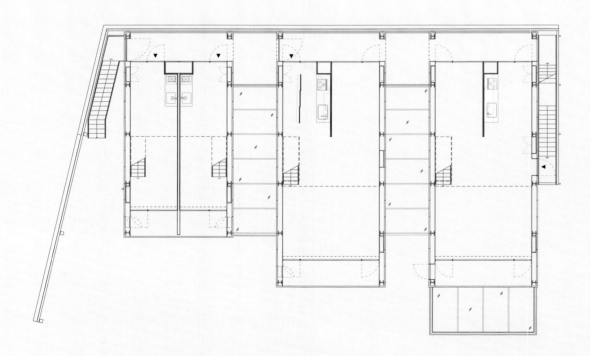

"We didn't want any grid or construction joints to show," Faulders recalls. "And there was no way you could have vertical columns pacing through this thing and holding it up. Working with a company over there, we developed a system of very thin steel rods that are suspended on supports from the top to bottom, so the structure evaporates."

41 Cooper Square
New York, New York

41 Cooper Square, the nine-story, full-block facility designed by Thom Mayne of Morphosis for the Cooper Union for the Advancement of Science and Art, answered a range of needs for the art, architecture, and engineering school in Manhattan's East Village. Because it replaced two preexisting structures housing different academic programs, says project architect Jean Oei, "it's an 'everything' building," adroitly combining laboratories, classrooms, studios, and public spaces in its 175,000 square feet. Morphosis accomplished this, moreover, on a relatively scant budget of about $650 per square foot—"really low for a lab building," Oei says.

Yet what most interested Mayne were 41 Cooper's social components, in terms of both the school's mission and the nature of academic life. Since its beginning in 1859—in the landmark (and, for its day, design-forward) Foundation Building just to the north—Cooper Union has provided full-tuition scholarships to every student, and Mayne wanted his design to reflect the institution's open-handedness with a transparency that, says Oei, "invites the community into the school and gives back energy to the city." More important—since the campus was downsizing and its three academic constituencies would be increasingly under one roof—the architect sought greater transparency between the disciplines, which made "the non-programmed spaces the most interesting part of the project," Mayne says. "Schools are not about transferring information—they're about the social development of young people as they mingle with other tribes. So we wanted to make a situation where the students would be cheek-by-jowl, like you are in New York City."

Mayne addressed the building's public aspect by cladding it in translucent, perforated metal panels. The skin "does a bunch of things," says Mayne: it provides solar shading and ventilation in summer and insulation in cold weather and is also, the architect notes, "dynamic in its relationship to light. It looks completely different from season to season and hour to hour"; highly transparent at night, "it becomes quite opaque and reflective at other times."

Because the shape of the building had been negotiated (based on zoning laws and community input) prior to Morphosis's involvement, "the skin also plays a powerful role in making that condition invisible—it doesn't look like we just got stuck with something," says the architect. "And it allowed me to suppress the traditional facade of solids and voids, and to be more conceptual: to shape the building to express what we wanted to express—its relationship to its surroundings—and open it where we wanted to open it." Mayne's opening—a T-shaped, multistory cut in the structure's undulating principal facade—"projects onto the outside a hint of what you're going to experience when you go in, which is the school's incredible human capital."

What the cut partly exposes is 41 Cooper's main event: a 135-foot-high atrium constructed from a four-story, twenty-foot-wide grand stair and two additional three-story switchback stairs accessed from the fifth- and eighth-floor elevator stops. This space—Mayne calls it "a vertical piazza"—winds up through the building's core to form a vast social arena in which students ceaselessly intermingle. Although a white lattice structure defines the atrium, it remains sufficiently porous to permit multiple views and opportunities for interaction across the stairs, as well as from level to level. And just as the building's facade engages with its surroundings and invites them in, the atrium creates an urban condition of its own that everywhere connects to the neighborhood through windows large and small. "No matter where you are, your experience refers to New York City," says Mayne.

Citing the exterior skin, hand-built atrium lattice, and radiant heating-and-cooling ceiling system, says the architect, "there's an incredible refinement in certain places." Yet the utilitarian material palette, including structural concrete and chain link and unadorned institutional classrooms and studios, conveys a surprising roughness, as though a postwar urban high school had been reimagined for the twenty-first century. "I wasn't happy with it at first," Mayne admits. "But that rawness really belongs in the East Village—it's another connection to the community."

2009
Morphosis Architects

Rather than creating an aggressive building, architect Thom Mayne explains, "I let the facade fold back in and it makes a huge difference." The structure's undulant main facade, which remains more orthogonal at its southern end, "transforms as it moves north—the entry lifts as it moves toward this lovely articulated baroque building at the corner."

"Everything is multivalent and has to do two or three things," says Mayne. "The first thing the skin does is take 50 percent of the heat out of the building in summer." Environmentally friendly—the first LEED-certified laboratory academic building in New York—the structure is also a good neighbor: concerns that the Ukrainian Catholic church just behind 41 Cooper would be less visible were addressed by creating a view cone through the structure's lower floor.

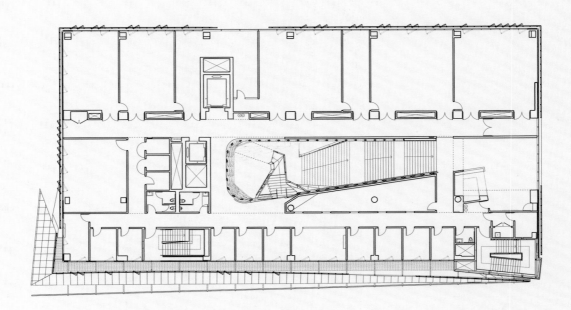

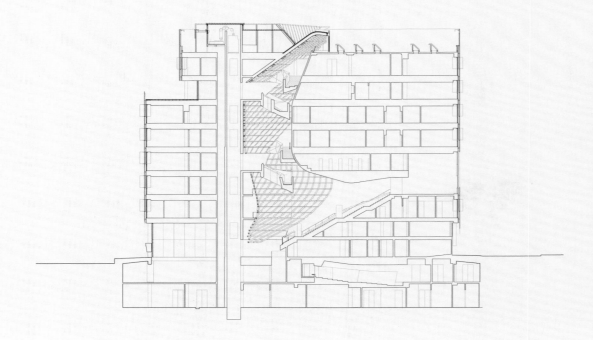

Operable panels in the building's facade help to ventilate heat in the warm months. Within, niches, seating areas, and heavy-use zones such as computer labs and locker rooms are strategically positioned at different levels, multiplying the opportunities for interaction. One of Mayne's seating areas makes a specific visual connection with Cooper Union's original Foundation Building, across Third Avenue to the north, tying together the two-building campus.

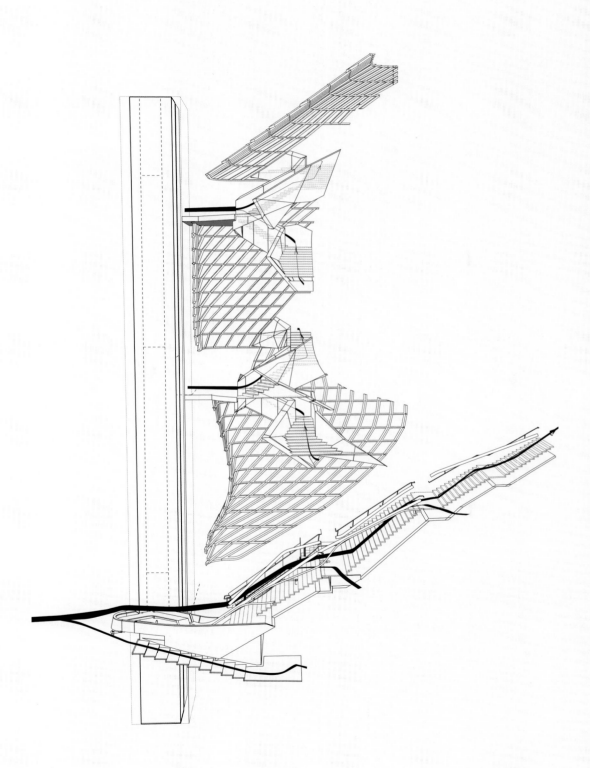

"It's an outdoor stair that's inside—a vertical piazza," says Mayne of the four-story, twenty-foot-wide grand stair that rises up from the building's main lobby. Students cluster on it at every level, which, the architect observes, is the point—"you couldn't have a Spanish Steps without human beings." The porous latticework structure loosely defining the atrium space permits views from level to level as well as to the outdoors.

Solar Umbrella
Venice, California

Lawrence Scarpa explains the residence he and Angela Brooks remodeled for themselves and their son as an attempt "to make a house that was more air than building." Partly this arose from aesthetics. "For me, structure isn't something to highlight—like lighting, it should just disappear," Scarpa observes. But it derived as well from the pleasures of Southern California living, and the desire to extract the most from them on a 4,000-square-foot through lot that—unusually for the area—spans two streets. "We wanted to make the house part of the yard," Scarpa says. "So we tried not to distinguish between them."

The family had resided in the single-story, two-bedroom 1920s bungalow, its front facade set roughly twelve feet from one of the streets bordering the property, under tight circumstances: 650 square feet (enlarged from 400 in the 1930s). Scarpa and Brooks added nearly twice that area and, critically, reversed the house's orientation; they placed an entry, living room, guest bath, and utility spaces onto what had been the rear of the bungalow and expanded upward into a new second-floor master suite—effectively converting the back yard into an expansive, enclosed front green. The directional change focused the building toward the south and facilitated the planar wrap of solar panels that climbs the southern facade and folds into a canopy—inspired by Paul Rudolph's 1953 Umbrella House in Sarasota, Florida—above the master suite. The gesture, notes Scarpa, "serves many purposes, aesthetically, functionally, and perceptually"—not least, providing the house with virtually all of its electricity.

Scarpa and Brooks employed multiple gambits to interconnect interior and exterior, notably in the entry procession, alongside a cast-in-place concrete pool: at the threshold, the water flows into a koi pond set with stepping stones that lead to the front door. The master suite, above the living room, is a small glass-enclosed sleeping area opening onto a patio "within the visual bounds of the building envelope"—a see-through outdoor space shaped by evanescent structural planes, including a distinctive "bristle broom" slatted screen. The glass living room wall can be completely opened to the yard; the glazed sliding panels are at grade and the interior space sits eighteen inches below it, says Scarpa, so "when you open the doors, the edge of the adjacent patio becomes one long bench where people can sit." When the glass panels are pocketed, he adds, "most people don't bother with the front door—they get sucked right into that big hole."

Although the design is complex—the relationships between the structure's built elements and void spaces are multifaceted and at times poetic—Scarpa and Brooks succeeded in creating an architecture that appears immaterial. "It's open, light-filled, there's lots of cross-ventilation," Scarpa observes. "And on both levels, you can see right through it."

2005
Pugh + Scarpa Architects

Angela Brooks and Lawrence Scarpa nearly tripled the size of their 650-square-foot bungalow and, critically, reversed its orientation so that the front of the house now overlooks what was previously the back yard. Pocket doors open the first-floor living room entirely to the outdoors; the second-floor master suite appears to be little more than horizontal and vertical planes—more the suggestion of structure than structure itself.

"When you're inside the living room looking toward the entry, it just looks like a wall of cabinetry," Scarpa says. "But the door to the entry is built into the cabinetry, and also the guest bathroom door is in a bookshelf that's integral with the cabinets."

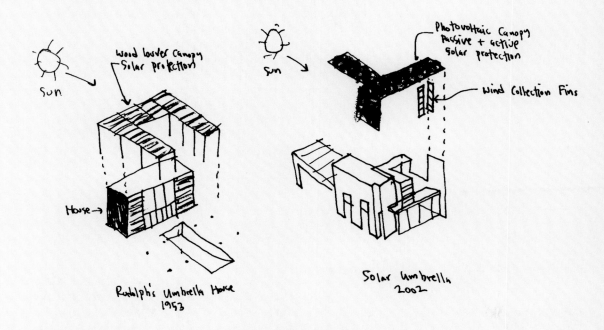

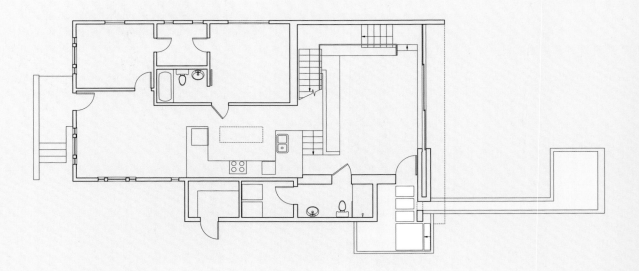

Glass Pavilion at the Toledo Museum of Art
Toledo, Ohio

When the Toledo Museum of Art selected Kazuyo Sejima and Ryue Nishizawa to design a pavilion to contain its glass collection—one of the world's finest—it was a remarkably prescient choice: their Tokyo-based firm SANAA, now a major international presence, had no built work outside Japan. "They said they chose us because, after visiting our buildings, they appreciated their quiet presence," says project architect Toshiko Oki.

Both actually and philosophically, the program—influenced by Toledo's history as a center of industrial and studio glass production—required more than object display. In the 1960s, the museum became one of the first institutions to establish a workshop for the creation of art glass, and the directors wanted to include new glassmaking facilities in the same structure as the collection. Moreover, Edward Drummond Libbey, who launched the Toledo glass industry in the 1880s, had established the museum in 1901 as a free institution, and the new pavilion, it was hoped, would express a comparable civic commitment.

SANAA's scheme—a 76,000-square-foot structure composed almost entirely of layers of curvilinear glass—might at first seem like a one-liner. In fact, says Oki, "the physical transparency was a way of achieving programmatic transparency." Enclosing gallery and workshop spaces in glass enables them to visually communicate; creating transparent galleries, Oki adds, "gives the curators different spatial proportions to work with, without having to leave the single large room, which is what gallery spaces tend to be." The museum's historic inclusiveness, he observes, was also rooted in transparency: "The pavilion is in a park—people can see in and feel a part of it."

After siting the workshop to the south and establishing that the exhibition spaces would skew toward the building's north side to avoid the damaging effects of sunlight, says Oki, "the plan went through hundreds of renditions." Starting as a traditional grid, the design gradually transformed as its creators struggled to craft individualized galleries that, even with the art extracted, might still express their spatial character. The structure's supple curves began with rounded corners, then extended throughout; the architects gently defined rooms and circulation areas so that the experience of passing from one to the next would seem fluid and inevitable rather than rigid. "If we had corners, the glass would feel harder and so would the building," Oki says. The narrow in-between zones that enable the spaces to, in Oki's formulation, "slide past each other" also equalize the environment by layering "invisible insulation" between different climates, including the galleries and public rooms, "hot shops" containing the glassmaking facilities, and the outdoors.

The "quiet presence" so admired by the museum's directors is everywhere present in SANAA's creation. "During the design phase there was worry that so much glass would make people feel bottled," Oki says. "But the experience is quite natural and changes constantly. At night, you can see straight through the building. But during the day, when you have reflections, the glass becomes a canvas, or the balance between inside and outside becomes more even"—especially because the design incorporates courtyards that bring daylight into the interior. The outcome is less a transparent building than transparency formed into narrative: about light, structure, nature, and, most of all, space—personal, communal, and the quicksilver zone in between.

2006
Kazuyo Sejima and
Ryue Nishizawa/SANAA

The museum's glassmaking facility, sited on the building's south side, is visible from both the park in which the pavilion sits and the exhibition and circulation spaces within the structure. "The studio glass movement partly comes from the Toledo Museum of Art," says project architect Toshiko Oki. "They wanted to continue this because it's the birthplace, and to create a place where local glass artisans could work."

SANAA developed numerous iterations of the plan as the firm struggled to answer programmatic demands and craft galleries that—even with the art removed—might still express their spatial character. "It was very important to open up courtyards," Oki explains. "Partly for a connection to the sky when you're deep in the building, but also to deal with glare. If there were no courtyards, you'd have a glare effect and the interior would be darker."

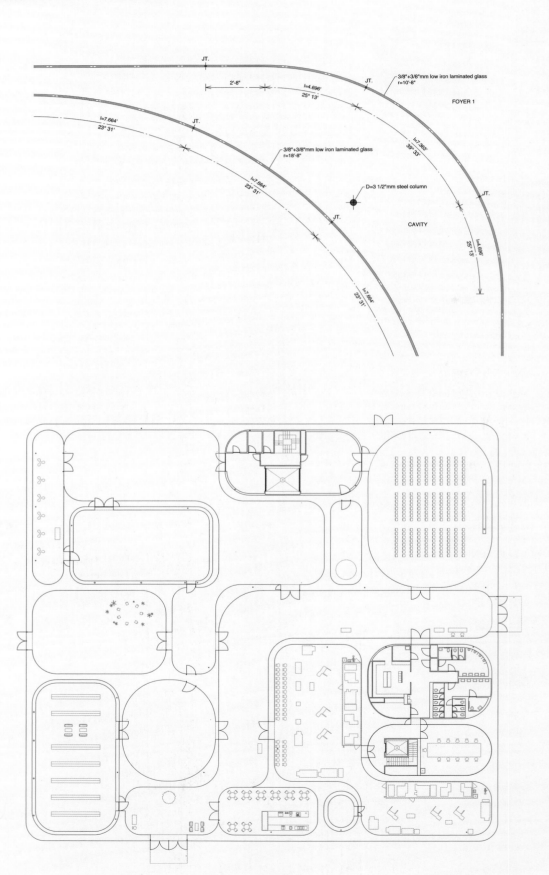

"What makes the building interesting is that it isn't transparent all the time," says Oki. "If it were, you would understand the building relatively quickly when you walked in. But because there's a level of complexity through the reflections on the glass, and in the way it captures the environment, the building always seems a little different every time you move through."

Acknowledgments

For the second time in two years, Gianfranco Monacelli and Andrea Monfried of The Monacelli Press have given me a free hand in the researching and writing of a book on a subject of my choosing, an opportunity for which I am grateful.

A special thank you to Rebecca McNamara, also of Monacelli, who managed the book's complicated process of creation, dealt patiently and graciously with complex personalities, and offered many useful observations regarding the text.

Claudia Brandenburg's design visualizes the book's theme with beauty and subtlety. An illustrated book is as much an aesthetic object as a literary one—if not more so—and I am fortunate to have so able and inspiring a creative partner.

My heartfelt thanks as well to the architects who permitted me to include their work—and took great pains to speak with me about it, often at length—and to the photographers whose images interpret that work with visual elegance and narrative intelligence.

I have, as always, relied on friends and colleagues to point me toward projects that spoke to the subject in interesting ways, and they have immeasurably enriched my work. To Adam Yarinsky, Stephen Cassell, Thom Faulders, Emily Nemens, Louise Harpman, and Yael Melamede: thank you.

It is often the case that one begins with a subject and, through the process of exploring it, refines or even redefines one's thinking about it. In this regard, my conversations with the architects Laura Briggs and Jonathan Knowles and the artist Nina Lora have been exceptionally instructive.

Finally, I must express my gratitude to my dear friend, tireless advocate, and indispensable advisor Jill Cohen. The only times Jill has failed me have been when I've failed to take her advice—which will never happen again.

Photography Credits

An architecture and design journalist, Marc Kristal is a contributing editor of *Dwell*, a former editor of *AIA/J*, and has written for *Metropolis*, the *New York Times*, *Architectural Digest*, *Elle Décor*, and numerous other publications. His most recent book is *Re:Crafted: Interpretations of Craft in Contemporary Architecture and Interiors*. In 2003, he curated the exhibition "Absence Into Presence: The Art, Architecture, and Design of Remembrance" at Parsons School of Design, and in 2009, he was part of the project team that created the Greenwich South planning study for the Alliance for Downtown New York. Also a screenwriter, Kristal wrote the film *Torn Apart*. He lives in New York.